DATE DUE

JAN 3 0 1997	

BRODART   Cat. No. 23-221

RA-CISM . . . the assumption that psycho-cultural traits and capacities are determined by biological race and that races differ decisively from one another which is usually coupled with a belief in the inherent superiority of a particular race and its right to domination over others.

Webster's Dictionary, 3rd Int'l. Edition

RACIAL DISCRIMINATION . . . "shall mean any distinction, exclusion, restriction or preference based on race, color, descent, or national or ethnic origin which has the purpose or effect of nullifying or impairing the recognition, enjoyment or exercise, on an equal footing, of human rights and fundamental freedoms in the political, economic, social, cultural or any other field of public life."

Article 1, UN International Convention on the Elimination of All Forms of Racial Discrimination

THE ANATOMY OF RACISM: CANADIAN DIMENSIONS

DAVID R.HUGHES
EVELYN KALLEN

 HARVEST HOUSE, MONTREAL

The Anatomy of Racism: Canadian Dimensions has been published with the help of a grant from the Social Science Research Council of Canada, using funds provided by the Canada Council.

The authors of *The Anatomy of Racism* are the recipients of the CANADIAN HUMAN RIGHTS FOUNDATION AWARD for 1973, given annually for the best book, film, play, or other project on the subject of human rights in Canada.

For information address Harvest House Ltd., 4795 St. Catherine Street West, Montreal H3Z 2B9, Canada.

Printed and bound in Canada.

Acknowledgements

The conceptual framework developed in Chapters 6 to 10 represents an attempt to synthesize and build upon ideas drawn largely from three works: Shibutani, T. & Kwan, K. (eds.), *Ethnic Stratification*, New York, Macmillan, 1967, for the overall framework of Chapters 6 to 10; Yetman, N. R. and Steele, C. H. (eds.), *Majority and Minority: The Dynamics of Racial and Ethnic Relations*, Boston, Allyn and Bacon, 1971, for the elaboration of forms of racism expressed in Chapter 6; Gordon, M., *Assimilation in American Life*, New York, O.U.P., 1964, for the analysis of assimilation processes and models of integration expressed in Chapter 9.

We are especially indebted to Ellen Baar, who painstakingly read and criticized an earlier draft of this book, and to Bella Cheung and Diana Abraham for their patient typing and retyping of the manuscript.

We should also like to express our gratitude to Mr. Gerald Schiff, of Kent, Connecticut, for his generous hospitality, extended to us during the labours of producing a final version of the book.

D. R. H.
E. K.

DAVID HUGHES

Born in North Wales and educated at Cambridge, David Hughes had broad teaching experience before he came to Canada, in places as far apart as Singapore, Borneo and Cambridge. An author of eleven books with extensive field work behind him, he was well-equipped to undertake *The Anatomy of Racism*.

In 1965, Hughes became head of the Physical Anthropology Section of the National Museum in Ottawa and, subsequently, assumed the posts of Professor of Anthropology and Chairman of the Department of Anthropology at the University of Toronto. As Director from 1968 of the Human Adaptability Project, Igloolik, N.W.T., Hughes was responsible for co-ordinating the research of a team of twenty scientists from five Canadian universities in a five-year programme. He is currently Chairman, International Study of Eskimos (Canada, U.S.A., France, Denmark, Finland, Sweden, Norway).

EVELYN KALLEN

A native Torontonian, Evelyn Kallen has an intimate understanding of social and racial problems particular to Canada. She has participated in many studies and taught university courses covering such varied topics as race and ethnic relations, minorities in Canada, social and cultural change and social anthropology of religion. Her other interests include adolescence and youth, Jewish community studies and, most recently, the Canadian Eskimo. Kallen seems to have an indefatigable source of energy, she not only holds a position as Associate Professor in the Department of Social Science at York University, but is also Chairman of the Faculty of Arts Curriculum Committee.

Some awards that Kallen has earned during her academic career include the Panhellenic Prize, Province of Ontario grant, and Canada Council Doctoral Fellowship. She has published widely on the subjects of her interest and is a contributor to two forthcoming volumes on Canadian minorities.

Introduction

The impetus for this book came originally from the teaching experiences of the authors but more particularly from the proceedings of a conference and "International workshop to combat racism and racial discrimination" held at Bergamo East (Conference centre) in Marcy, New York State, during the month of October, 1971; the conference was sponsored jointly by the Canadian and U.S. commissions on UNESCO and the National Councils of Christians and Jews of Canada and the U.S.A. The authors were invited to present their views on race and racism to the participants, who were drawn from many concerned communities and from many walks of life in both countries. Accordingly, one author (D. R. H.) spoke of the biological scientist's attitude towards the concept of race and of the doubtful validity of many of the criteria commonly used to distinguish between, and to classify mankind. Particular emphasis was laid upon the zoological unity of our contemporary human species together with the mechanism underlying its evolution, and the incongruity of many current and misguided attempts to align the biological and social aspects of mankind. The other author (E. K.) was charged with explaining the social scientist's approach to the concepts of race and racism, and with attempting to eradicate some of the misconceptions arising from the misuse of the socially-defined concept of race for invidious political purposes. Special attention was paid to the function of racism together with negative racial stereotypes in rationalizing the status quo within an ethnically stratified society and to the strategies, predicated on the enforcement of human rights legislation, whereby structural racism might be eliminated.

From the prolonged discussions that followed, it appeared to the authors that much well-intentioned argument was weakened in its effectiveness by an apparent lack of awareness as to how these two kinds of data—the biological and the social—were interrelated. In the Canadian context, too, the lack of a unified and concise body of reference data and of models explained in Canadian terms was a constant frustration. Most of the existing texts drawn upon in discussion dealt with examples based on experience in the United States or in countries such as South Africa.

Following the conference, therefore, a suggestion by our editor and fellow conferee, Maynard Gertler, that a Canadian-oriented book on the subject of race and racism would be timely and useful prompted the authors to expand their thoughts and put them down on paper. The result is this volume; its main purpose is to try and illuminate some of the background of our contemporary struggle for human rights and fundamental freedoms in Canada, and to draw together relevant argument and data from Canadian and other sources.

Igloolik, N.W.T., 1972
Lake Kashagawigamog, Ont., 1973

Contents

Chapter 1

The Spectrum of Man
and His Diversity

As has been indicated in the foregoing Introduction, this book is written to clarify the distinctions and connections that can be made between the two concepts "race" and "racism".

We must, however, from the outset emphasize the difference in the nature of the material that is dealt with in describing these two concepts. This is important because much of our day-to-day contact with the subject—in conversation, in reading, from radio, television, newspapers, magazines and so on—presupposes that the two concepts are virtually identical, and that their evidence and arguments are mutually supportive.

On the other hand, there has been in recent years enough publicity about the subject, and enough expression of different opinions, scientific and otherwise, to make more and more people aware that the customary social concept of race is not valid in terms that are used by most anthropologists today.

Anthropology as a scientific discipline is becoming inevitably more and more specialized in its methods and subject matter, and one convenient division of interests is between regarding man as a member of the animal kingdom, a biological species, and as a social animal or species with impressions, attitudes and values drawn from the groups or populations into which it has become assembled. At many points, of course, these two kinds of interests overlap.

That part of anthropology that is mainly concerned with inquiry into the scientific nature of race (as opposed to racism) is called "physical anthropology", or, more frequently today, "human biology". What is not generally realized, however, is that in recent years physical anthropologists themselves have begun to question more closely whether this concept of "race" is in fact a valid one at all, and this doubt is echoed by many of their colleagues in other biological sciences (Count 1950; Mayr, 1963).

This part of the book therefore is an attempt to set out some of the scientific evidence related to the concept of "race" referred to immediately above in an effort to clear up misunderstandings that have arisen, and which still exist. It is these misunderstandings, some unintentional and some deliberate, that have often influenced both proponents and opponents of attitudes towards mankind that are commonly referred to as "racism".

To understand the nature of the scientific evidence, then, one must grasp some of the facts concerning man as a biological species. These facts will supply the answers (sometimes still incomplete) to such crucial questions as where did man evolve and why? What do we know of the story of his development from earliest times to the present day? When did the concept of "race" first enter into human thinking? What did it mean in the past and what does it mean today? Are all men born equal? How did the visible differences between us—in the colour of skin, hair and eyes, for example—come about? What do they mean? Are there really invisible differences between us—for example in intelligence, physical energy and stamina, blood group systems, physiology—that can be demonstrated in unemotional scientific terms?

The examination of these questions, and many other similar ones, is the opening purpose of this book.

DEFINING THE TERM "RACE"

The word "race" first occurs in the English language about A.D. 1500. A study of its etymology shows that it was adopted from the French word *race*, which is connected to the Italian *razza* and the Spanish *raza*. Beyond this, the origin of the word is lost in obscurity.

The initial usage of the word in English was apparently to indicate a class or set of persons (or even plants and animals) possessing some common feature or features. This might be common descent or origin. In the sixteenth century the term race was used more widely, and could mean the people of a house, or a family, as well as a tribe, nation or people regarded as being of common stock.

It was not until the eighteenth century however that the term was used to indicate one of the major divisions of mankind showing certain physical characteristics (such as skin colour) in common. Whilst in earlier usage the term had generally been used to mean "the human race", "the race of men" or "the race of mankind", its later meaning grew more narrow and particularly as the voyages of explorers and the journals of travellers revealed more and more of the physical varieties of mankind.

By the middle of the nineteenth century English usage of the term had come to include conditions or qualities resulting from belonging to a particular people or ethnic stock. Groups of several tribes or peoples were considered as making up these distinct ethnic stocks or races. This connecting of physical attributes with behavioural and other cultural attributes was to persist into modern times, and remains a common belief today.

CLASSIFICATION AND "RACE"

It had long been realized by early scholars such as Aristotle and by the later mediaeval thinkers that any attempt to understand the earth and its animals and plants required some system or systems of classification and description. From this attempt were to emerge the fields of study variously known as systematics and taxonomy.

These studies were concerned with sorting out things seen in nature into various categories, with pigeon-holing the phenomena of the natural world. Plants and herbs, for example, were studied from the aspect of their appearance and value for medical purposes. From these observations arose some of our earliest systematic classifications, the medicinal pharmacopoeias. Inevitably, confusion arose as different students attempted different systems and often used different criteria from those of their colleagues.

The Swedish botanist Carl Linné, or Carolus Linnaeus (1701-1778), was the first scientist of his time to bring order to this nomenclatural and systematic confusion. He took upon himself the task of classifying the whole of living nature, first publishing his scheme in 1735 under the title *Systema Naturae*. His revisions appeared in subsequent editions of the book, culminating in an elaborated version —the Tenth Edition, published in 1758. In this edition he applied a binomial system of nomenclature to the entire animal kingdom. Each creature was attributed with its fellows to a *species*, and each *species* was identified by two names viz. *genus* and *species* (hence "binomial"). The generic name appeared with its first letter in capitals, whilst the second or specific name appeared in lower-case letters. This apparently simple system was adopted with alacrity by the scientists of Linnaeus' time, as they immediately grasped its obvious advantages. As a taxonomic system it remains with us today, although from time to time revisions of particular classifications have been made. The terms *genus* and *species* had been used before Linnaeus' great contribution, but he was the first to put forward clear definitions as to how they might most profitably be utilized.

The adoption of Linnaeus' system greatly encouraged the inquiries of biological scientists and there was an expansion of efforts to classify all organic forms of life. It was soon realized that some taxonomic term below the species level was needed to fulfil this task. Terms such as "race", "variety" and "sub-species" were adopted from older usage, and pressed into use. It should be emphasized, however, that such terms have been variously defined, both then and now, and frequently have little exactitude beyond an understanding that they refer to one category or another below the species level.

Today, there is a general scientific acceptance that all contemporary mankind belongs to the same biological species: *Homo sapiens*. It follows, therefore, that any further subdivisions into peoples, populations, tribes, stocks, types and races can only be justified (if at all) on this sub-specific level. But as we look at man's past we become aware of significant differences between man today and his earlier ancestors, and these differences are sufficient (as we shall see later) to justify distinguishing between different species and even genera of man.

One important criterion in defining a species is that it has reproductive or genetic unity. Members of a species, therefore, are interfertile. They may mate with one another without hindrance if given the opportunity. In some cases, of course, geographical barriers or distance may preclude such mating opportunities; thus there are no recorded instances, for example, of Eskimos mating with Australian aborigines or with Kalahari Bushmen. On the other hand, there are numerous examples of "exotic" matings within the human species (for instance, between Chinese or Japanese and Negroes) that, in biological terms at any rate, have resulted in no deleterious effects. We may confidently assert therefore that because of this circumstance there is no basic biological or genetical difference between the various populations making up our contemporary species. Differences such as skin, hair and eye colour, therefore, have no bearing upon human reproductive abilities. We shall see later that such superficially obvious physical characteristics do not display discrete boundaries between populations. The tendency rather is for them to grade imperceptibly from one category to another across a continent. Gross differences, where they do exist, can be explained by abrupt barriers such as intervening oceans, or by deliberate migrations of groups of mankind in response to pressures of various kinds.

PAST AND PRESENT CLASSIFICATIONS OF MANKIND

We have seen that the first serious attempt at the systematic classification of living things was made by Linnaeus. In 1745, he proposed from his study of living man that four main races could be said to exist—Europeans, Asiatics, Africans and American Indians. Linnaeus' criteria for this division were skin colour (i.e. White, Yellow, Black and Brown) and subjective assessments of what he considered from observation to be the behavioural characteristics of each of these races. The term he preferred for these sub-specific units was *varieties*, but his precise definition of this term is not clear.

In 1781, a German physiologist, Johann Friedrich Blumenbach, who was much interested in the scientific study of mankind, proposed a classification of man based on head shape or skull shape. His division was into five races called by him Caucasian (i.e. European), Negro, Mongol, Malayan and American Indian. To the scientists of his day his categories had the merit of depending upon an objective criterion, head shape, whilst agreeing with the very visible distinctions between white, black, yellow, brown and "red" skin colour. They also avoided the subjectivity that accompanied some of Linnaeus' earlier criteria.

Following Blumenbach there were to be many modifications of these apparently basic divisions of mankind. Most of these modifications involved the addition of further criteria for differentiating between various major populations of mankind as the science of the measurement of man, and that of the observation of his physical characteristics, developed and advanced. The measurement of living man is now referred to as "anthropometry" or, if skeletal evidence is being considered, "osteometry". Many characteristics of living man are not subject to precise measurement: for example, the type of hair (woolly, curly, wavy, straight), and the shape of such features as the eyelids, lips, ears, or the colour of a person's eyes. The methods of recording such observations are referred to as "anthroposcopy" and by their very nature are more sub-jective criteria than precise metrical data.

During the eighteenth and nineteenth centuries the classification of mankind into "races" of various kinds was to become an obsession with the physical anthropologists of the day, and divisions and sub-divisions proliferated with every new discovery of hitherto undescribed indigen-ous populations. The French scientist Paul Broca was one very active worker of this period and was to exert great influence in the classification of mankind. Another French worker was Joseph Deniker who devised an elaborate system that included no less than ten "races" to be found within the geographical boundaries of Europe.

What was the purpose of this obsessive search for significant classifications of the world's peoples? We should remember, first of all, that these systems were initiated by European scientists. Naturally enough, they wished to compare the peoples they encountered or read about with their own populations. They were impressed by the appar-ent differences between human populations—differences that many assumed to have been preordained by some Divine Maker. Thus, differences were understood to rep-resent rigid immutable divisions within mankind, and inevitably many scientists sought to arrange these "races" in some hierarchical order ranging from "primitive" to "highly civilized". This, in turn, was understood by many as implying that some "races" were superior to others and that some therefore were preordained to be "inferior". The usual yardstick was achievement in a material and "cultural" sense, allied to a theological dogmatism that invariably placed Christianity higher than Paganism. Many indigenous peoples, when discovered by European explorers and travellers, were considered to be living in isolation, and this circumstance encouraged the prevailing idea that such "races" were "pure" and therefore unique divisions of man, unrelated to other groups of mankind.

We should remember, of course, that these earlier scholars had no knowledge of the science of human genetics that today exerts so important an influence upon consideration of what is meant by "race". Beginning with the discoveries of Gregor Mendel (1822-1884), Abbott of Brünn, and subsequently elaborated by innumerable workers, the science of genetics was to revolutionize man's thinking about himself and about the interrelationship between all human populations. At the same time interest in the skeletal remains of earlier man became widespread, scientifically respectable, and objective in research techniques. Slowly, the story of the evolution of man into today's diversity of peoples unfolded.

Are these earlier classifications to be dismissed today as being misguided and entirely irrelevant? Let us suppose that we have a roomful of miscellaneous students drawn from some large Canadian university such as the University of Toronto. Such a group will contain men and women from a variety of "ethnic" backgrounds. Although the majority will be Canadian by citizenship (and thus British subjects), there will be in the room students who are quite "obviously" of Chinese or of Negro family background. That is to say, upon superficial examination, these students will stand out from their "European" companions, and may also be distinguished (by group) from one another. Many of us, however, will be unable to distinguish between a Canadian Chinese and a Canadian Japanese, or between a Canadian Negro with an African family background and one whose family migrated here from the Caribbean. We could confidently assume, however, that any intelligent child invited into the room could rapidly distinguish (on a basis of skin colour) between the "major divisions" of mankind that were represented within the student body.

Let us suppose, after this demonstration of the apparent "sorting value" of one physical characteristic, that we take a small sample of blood from each student present and submit this to the human biologist in some anonymous laboratory with the request that he distinguish by his tests between blood derived from "Chinese", "Negro" and "European" students. Although not impossible, this would be a difficult task, particularly if the scientist was restricted in his tests to those involving only the blood group systems. Even if he were completely successful, which is doubtful, he would have expended far more laboratory time and effort in securing a result that the previously mentioned child might have obtained in a very few minutes.

Table 1: *Hooton's Sorting Criteria to Distinguish Between Three Primary Divisions of Living Mankind.* *

Criteria	Caucasoid or Europiform	Negroid or Negriform	Mongoloid or Mongoliform
Skin Colour	White, pink or "ruddy" to light brown	Dark brown to black	Yellow or yellow-brown
Eye Colour	All lighter shades, but never black	Dark brown to black	Medium brown to dark brown
Hair Type	Straight to wavy, occasionally curled	Woolly to frizzy; oval in cross-section	Straight (coarse in texture), and circular in cross-section
Nose Shape	Usually high-bridged and narrow	Usually low or depressed, broad tip and nostrils	Low root, short tip, medium width at nostrils
Lip Shape	Thickness, medium to thin; little or no lip eversion†	Usually thick with obvious eversion	Medium thickness; variable eversion
Cheek-bone Region	Not prominent	Variable, but usually more obvious than in Caucasoid	Projecting forwards and laterally; may be covered by fat pad
Body Hair (including beard)	Medium to heavy; very variable	Medium to scanty	Usually less than Caucasoid or Negroid

* Modified from Hooton's *Up From the Ape* (1946).
† Turning upwards and downwards of external lip margins.

The fuller reasons for what may at first appear to be a disappointing comparison of methods will be discussed later, but one difference in the two procedures can be mentioned here. The child, inspecting one student after another is employing a gross but effective screening technique on an individual student basis. The human biologist, however, is more accustomed to dealing with *populations* of mankind, and the *frequencies* of particular blood groups within samples of such populations. Thus, a Canadian of Italian descent and one of African Negro descent might both possess blood of Group A (within the ABO system). It would not serve by itself, therefore, to distinguish between them.

Again, peoples such as the Chinese (and related peoples such as Japanese or Koreans) often possess in their blood a substance identified as the Diego antigen. However, not *all* Chinese possess this antigen. Thus a student from our sample whose blood revealed the presence of this Diego antigen would almost certainly be of Chinese or related extraction, but the *absence* of this Diego antigen could not automatically be assumed to indicate that the student was *not* a representative of the Mongoloid major division of mankind.

It will be obvious, then, from the foregoing example, that for certain purposes some of the earlier traditional sorting criteria still have their uses in particular situations. However, we will see upon further reflection that such criteria as were used by our "intelligent child" have their limitations. The difficulty he might experience in distinguishing between Japanese and Chinese, and so on, has already been mentioned. Utilizing skin colour alone, he might also be confused if confronted with a "black" Negro student and a "black" Asian Indian student. Clearly skin colour alone is not enough. Many Australian Aborigines and Papuans (of New Guinea) can also be considered to be "black", but cannot be realistically grouped within the same "race" as African Negroes. If this *were* done on these grounds, then it would make just as good sense to invent "races" of red-haired men or of freckled blonde women.

To return then to our original question: what is the value, if any, of these criteria based upon the inspection of superficial but very visible physical characteristics? Without question, as we increase the number and variety of these somewhat subjective criteria, the efficiency of the sorting procedure *into major* or *primary divisions of mankind* increases. So, today, such criteria still have value although they are usually used in conjunction with more objective criteria such as those derived from blood or other biochemical samples.

The American physical anthropologist Earnest Hooton drew up an expanded list of physical criteria of this kind that distinguishes reasonably well between three primary divisions of mankind. This appears in tabular form below, and has frequently been used as a basis of more recent sorting systems (Table 1).

Hooton then proceeded to subdivide these primary divisions, and sought to account for many "intermediate" types of mankind by mixture at various levels between representatives of his major groups. It is at this point that such systems depart from their attempts at objectivity, and become what are virtually academic exercises in taxonomy, often based on conjecture regarding human migration and past and present-day hybridizations. Such systems, then, as has been emphasized before, are of limited help in classifying mankind. They can only be of value when used in conjunction with other and more objective kinds of population "markers", such as are indicated in Table 4.

Man is and always has been an extremely mobile animal. In earlier days, of course, his numbers were more limited than they are today, but as the world population increased, his distribution expanded rapidly to all parts of the world. This can be briefly indicated in the following table, which sums up current estimates. Precise figures are obviously difficult to obtain, especially as one goes backward in time.

An examination of Table 2, remembering again that the figures listed can only be estimates, underlines the fact that this human species of ours has become increasingly mobile and increasingly successful in reproductive terms as it has evolved over the past million years or so. Man, as we shall see, appears further back than that point in time, but his earlier skeletal remains are few and fragmentary. As man has increased in numbers and in density, so he has diversified through breeding, sometimes in isolation

Table 2: *Past, Present and Projected Growth and Distribution of Human Populations.*

Approximate Years before Present	Culture Type	Population Estimate (millions)	World Areas(s) Occupied	Estimated World Density of Population (per square mile)
1,000,000	Palaeolithic or Old Stone Age	0.125	Asia and Africa	0.0112
300,000	Mesolithic or Middle Stone Age	1.00	Africa Europe and Asia	0.032
40,000	Neolithic or New Stone Age	3.34	Africa Europe and Asia	0.105
10,000		7.50	also New World and Australia	0.35
6,000	Rural farming and early urban	80.0	as for Neolithic	2.76
2,000	Rural farming and increased urban development	135.0	as for Neolithic	3.8
300	Farming, urban and industrial	545.0	World-wide	9.7
200		800.0		14.5
100		1300.0		22.0
Today		3000.0	(including Antarctica)	44.0
A.D. 2000?		?6300		?125.0

and sometimes through interbreeding between groups
(hybridization or miscegenation).

What then can the skeletal evidence of man earlier than
ourselves tell us about the origin of these primary divisions
of mankind and of the many varieties or types of human
population that we can observe around us today?
There is a basic difference between the kind of evidence
that we can draw from skeletal evidence of earlier man,
and that drawn from our visual and laboratory examination of the living. For example, bones recovered from the
ground can tell us nothing about skin, hair or eye colour
of the person they represent. We can say nothing about lip
shape or ear shape and very little about the probable shape
of the nose. Although attempts have been made to ascer-
tain the presence of blood group antigens from early human
bones the results must be dismissed as inconclusive. We
can say something about the state of health of earlier man
if the diseases or nutritional deficiencies that he may have
suffered from leave tell-tale marks on his bones and teeth
(e.g. arthritis or dental caries). We can say something
about the sex, age at death, stature, and so on, of individuals represented by bony remains. If we are experienced
in having looked at extensive collections of human remains
of known origin (identifiable by cultural evidence unearthed by the archaeologist) then it is often possible to
make an assessment of at least major or primary "racial"
affinities. Looking back in this way, then, we can attempt,
in very simple primary terms, to find out when and where
people corresponding to today's major world populations
first emerged upon the scene, and what their subsequent
population movements have been. Let us see next what
kinds of skeletal features can assist the investigators in
this task. Following Hooton again, some of the relevant
criteria are listed in Table 3.

There will of course be many exceptions to a simple
sorting procedure of this kind, and analysis will include
detailed measurements of all the bones, as such objective
metrical data can be very informative. The bones of many
Canadian Indians, for example, will show brow ridges as

prominent, or more prominent, than those of many Europeans, also their limb bones may be thicker and strongly marked at the sites of muscle attachments. This is despite the fact that American Indians in general are considered to fall within the primary or major Mongoloid division.

Let us look finally at frequency data relating to some commonly used genetic markers. What kinds of primary "racial" divisions can be made, using this kind of information alone, disregarding the physical appearance of the

Table 3: *Some Skeletal Characteristics Considered Typical of Three Primary Divisions of Mankind.*

Criteria	Caucasoid or Europiform	Negroid or Negriform	Mongoloid or Mongoliform
Features of the Skull	Brow ridges more developed than in Negroids or Mongoloids; mastoid process large	Forehead often rounded or globular; skull long in shape; prominent occipital area	Negligible development of brow ridges; flat occipital area, often with marked ridge; often a keel-shaped cranial vault
Facial Features	Straight (vertical) facial profile; small jaws, prominent chin	Prognathism (upper and lower jaws projecting); small chin; long narrow palate	Prominent cheek bones; wide lower jaw
Nasal Features	High narrow nasal bones	Low broad nasal bridge, and broad nasal aperture	Root of nose flat and broad; narrow nasal aperture
Long Bone Features	Thickly constructed; large joints with strong bony muscle markings	Slender bones; forearm and lower leg bones relatively longer than lower arm and upper leg bones	Generally intermediate between Negroid and Caucasoid with respect to these characters

Table 4: *Three Primary Divisions of Mankind and Their Relative Frequencies for Certain Blood Group Substances.*

Blood Group System	Gene	Caucasoid or Europiform	Negroid or Negriform	Mongoloid or Mongoliform
ABO	A_2	Moderate	Moderate	(virtually) Absent
	B	Low	Intermediate	High
RH or (Rhesus)	R^0	Low	High	Low
	r	High	Intermediate	(virtually) Absent
Duffy	Fy^2	Intermediate	Low	High
	Fy	Absent	High	Absent
Diego	Di^2	Absent	Absent	High
Sutter	Js^a	Absent	High	Absent

population samples being tested? Some relative frequencies are listed in Table 4 and all refer to well-known blood group systems that occur in man. The symbols under the heading "Gene" are conventional scientific shorthand notations for the genetic unit responsible for the presence or absence of a particular blood group antigen.

It is clear again from the genetic data in Table 4, that these primary divisions of mankind are distinguishable from one another if a battery of tests of this size is employed. The evidence of physical features, skeletal features and many genetic markers seems, therefore, to indicate clearly that these are differences between indigenous peoples of the same human species that are drawn from the three major geographical "breeding grounds" of human populations—that is Africa, Asia and Europe.

Obviously more precise information regarding the frequency of genetic markers is available than is conveyed by the terms high, intermediate and low in Table 4, which are merely employed to summarize what we know. The U.S. scientist A. S. Wiener, using genetical data of this kind, from the ABO and Rhesus systems, proposed in

1948 a classification of the world's living populations into six major groups. This was also the basic number proposed by another U.S. worker, W. C. Boyd, in 1950. Boyd distinguished between the following genetically-defined "races".

1. *Early European* (represented by the Basques of the Franco-Spanish border region)
2. *European*
3. *African*
4. *Asian*
5. *American Indian*
6. *Australian Aborigine*

Later workers such as U.S. scientists T. Dobzhansky, in 1962, and R. A. Goldsby, in 1971, sought to combine the information derived from genetic markers with that drawn from metrical and morphological observations. Each identified about 30 different types of mankind in this way. The kinds of differences they point out are those which exist between, say, Canadian Eskimos and Canadian Indians (both conventionally regarded as Mongoloids or Mongoliforms) or between Canadians of Scandinavian and of Italian origins (both conventionally regarded as Caucasoids or Europiforms).

A most useful hierarchy within classifications of mankind was introduced by S. M. Garn, whose 3rd Edition of *Human Races* appeared in 1971. Garn distinguishes between:

1. *Geographical races*: major human populations corresponding to the continental regions of the world.
2. *Local races*: large or small human populations, being sub-divisions of geographical races, and usually found within the boundaries of a continental region. These could be numbered in the hundreds.
3. *Micro-races*: much smaller human populations, often living (and therefore breeding) in partial isolation from other human groups. Boundaries

might not be geographical but religious, linguistic or other cultural ones. These micro-races could be numbered in the thousands.

It should be borne in mind, of course, that what are virtually new "races" of man have been evolving as the species has become increasingly mobile. What has been happening is an interchange of genetic material through hybridization and rehybridization. The "gene pools" originally characteristic of certain human populations have accordingly been modified by today in their composition. This brings not only variation in the frequencies of certain genetic markers, but also variation in external physical features. Examples of such comparatively "new" populations are numerous on the world scene.

The American Black is one such hybrid population. Historic and genetic evidence indicates that the American Black is the product mainly of African Black and European hybridization. The human geneticist, T. E. Reed of the University of Toronto has demonstrated this by analysis of frequency data relating to the presence of Duffy blood group antigens in American Blacks, African Blacks (from regions of Africa where Blacks were originally forced to migrate to the Americas) and American Whites (Caucasoids). His data are summarized below in Table 5. Note that in the earlier Table 4, Duffy positive (Fy) is shown as "low" in frequency in Negroid peoples taken as a whole and that it is of "intermediate" frequency in Caucasoids in general.

It is clear from this table that there has been a contribution of Duffy positive antigen genes to the American Black gene pool. Having utilized analysis of other blood group systems as well, Reed further estimates this Caucasoid genetic contribution in percentage terms as follows: to American Blacks as a whole 21.0; to American Blacks in Charleston, S. Carolina, 4.0; in two counties of Georgia 11.0; in Oakland, California 22.0; in Detroit, Michigan 26.0; in New York City 19.0.

Other new "races" of mankind formed in the same hybrid manner are: the Cape Coloured of South Africa

Table 5: *Duffy Antigen Frequencies in Selected Population Samples.* *

African Blacks from	Percentage of Duffy Positive
Upper Volta	0
Accra (Ghana)	0
Lagos (Nigeria)	0
Dahomey	0

American Blacks from	
South Carolina	3.7
Georgia	4.5
California (Oakland)	9.4
Michigan (Detroit)	11.1
New York City	8.1

American Blacks Considered Together	9.2
Caucasoids (Ancestral Origin Western Europe)	43.0

*Data from Reed, T. E., *Science*, 165 (1969), p. 762.

(representing a gene pool drawn from Bushmen-Hottentots, Bantus, Europeans, Malaysians and Asian Indians); the Ladino of South and Central America (genes from southern Europeans and southern Amerindians); and the Neo-Hawaiian (genes from northwest and southern Europeans, Polynesians, Chinese, Japanese and Filipinos); and the Métis of Canada (with genes from Cree, Sowto, Blackfoot, Chipewyan, Dogrib and Slavey Indians, and from Europeans from France and Scotland).

In the past it was considered by many writers that hybrid populations fell below the levels of fertility, intelligence and achievement of the two parental stocks. This is now clearly held to be erroneous, and the viability of many of these new "races" is proof of this. What has varied in the past and present is social recognition of such hybrids and the socio-economic opportunities offered to them.

Chapter 2

The Evolution of Man
and the Origin of "Races"

Canada's first peoples were the Indians and, much later, the Eskimos. Subsequently there arrived peoples from Europe such as the early Norsemen of Scandinavia, and the British and French. Today there are peoples from many other parts of Europe and many other parts of the world living in Canada.

It is important to remember that none of these peoples, even the Indians and Eskimos, *originated* in Canada, or even elsewhere in the Americas. The Americas, like Australia, are parts of the world most recently inhabited by man. Man evolved elsewhere in our world; there is evidence, for example, that he may have existed in Africa for more than 3 million years. In the Americas however, he is a newcomer by comparison, having probably only been here for some 40,000 years. It now appears certain that these earliest immigrants came from Asia.

Let us consider next, then, the evidence of the gradual evolution of man from non-human ancestors culminating with his differentiation, probably about 50,000 years ago, into what may be termed the primary or major divisions of mankind and, further, the mechanism that has brought this evolution and differentiation about.

The problem of the evolution of man has preoccupied

scholars for many centuries. Few subjects have provoked more controversy in the history of science. Religious dogma hindered early speculations as to man's origins but even more constraining was, until fairly recently, the lack of adequate skeletal and cultural evidence from which the story could be pieced together.

Linnaeus stressed the unique position of man within the Animal Kingdom. In his *Systema Naturae* (Tenth Edition, 1758), he developed a classificatory system into which all animals could be placed. Above the *species* level lay the *genera*. Above the *genera* lay *families*, *orders*, and *classes* in that sequence. Classes were grouped into *phyla*, 22 of which made up the Animal Kingdom. Linnaeus placed man within the order *Primates* together with his immediate relatives the apes, monkeys, lemurs and tarsiers. His criteria for grouping together these non-human creatures with man were characteristics such as forward-looking eyes (implying stereoscopic vision), five digits on each hand and foot, a single pair of mammary glands, convoluted well-developed brains, and so on. Within the sub-Order *Anthropoidea* he placed monkeys, apes and man, as they were more "man-like" than the lemurs and tarsiers. Recognizing next that apes were closer to man than the monkeys he placed the two in a super-Family *Hominoidea*, pointing out, amongst other criteria, that both were tailless, much larger than most monkeys, and generally more terrestrial in life habits.

Appreciating, however, that there were still considerable evolutionary differences between the apes and man, Linnaeus placed the latter in a category of its own, the Family *Hominidae*, with the apes in another, the Family *Pongidae*. Speaking colloquially then, it is convenient to refer to living man and his man-like ancestors as homin*ids*, to living apes and ancestral ape-like creatures as pong*ids* and to creatures resembling both apes and man as homin*oids*. Similarly anthrop*oids* is used to refer collectively to monkeys, apes and man.

The hominids include at least two genera, *Australopithecus* (appearing probably more than 3 million years ago, and now extinct) and *Homo* (appearing at least 600,000 years ago and perhaps as long ago as 1.5 million years). Some controversy exists as to whether there should be other earlier genera included within the hominids. The genus *Homo* is divided into two species: *H. erectus*, and *H. sapiens*. The former probably evolved about 600,000 years ago and the latter about 250,000 years ago. A third species, *H. habilis*, has also been proposed in recent years and may go back as far as 1.5 million years.

All contemporary mankind belongs to the species *Homo sapiens*. Although *H. sapiens* apparently appeared in Europe some 250,000 years ago, its resemblance at that time to modern man is largely confined to brain size. It is not until about 50,000 years ago that we find remains of *H. sapiens* whose facial and other bony morphology resemble that of groups of contemporary mankind.

THE EMERGENCE OF THE HOMINIDS

The hominoids are supposed to have split into the hominids and pongids about 15 to 20 million years ago. The problem of pinpointing in time and space the earliest existence of a hominid is crucial therefore in beginning the story of the evolution of man as we know him today.

Since 1934 scientists had been aware of the remains of a fossil primate, called generically *Ramapithecus*, which had flourished in the Siwalik Hills of N. W. India about 10 to 14 million years ago. The original discoverer of this find, G. E. Lewis, had been convinced that of many ancestral ape-like forms discovered by them from this period, *Ramapithecus* was the most man-like. Generally, until the 1960's, such a suggestion was received with polite scientific scepticism. Over the past decade or so, however, further finds attributable to *Ramapithecus* have been made, and intensive study by E. H. Simons and D. R. Pilbeam of Yale University (1965; 1972) have convinced many students of man's origins that *Ramapithecus* may well have been the first hominid so far discovered. If this is indeed so, then the genus should clearly belong within the Family *Hominidae*. Further finds in East Africa (at Fort

Ternan, Kenya) under the direction of the late L. S. B. Leakey, appear to resemble *Ramapithecus* very closely, and have been dated radio-metrically at 14 million years old, thus being contemporaneous with the finds in India, or possibly even a little earlier. It should be noted however, that both the African and Indian evidence consists only of teeth and some supporting jaw bones. We still know nothing of the general skeletal characters of the creature, and nothing of the size and shape of its skull. There is no cultural evidence, such as artefacts or remains of animal bones, to suggest that *Ramapithecus* was a hunter.

The next stage in the development of man is the emergence in Africa of the genus *Australopithecus*. A tantalizing gap exists in the hominid record, however, as it is not until about 5 million years ago that these creatures apparently appeared on the scene. A large number of fossil finds of *Australopithecus* has now been unearthed, mainly in South and East Africa, with some isolated finds in Asia that may also represent this genus. The genus is usually divided into two species *A. robustus* and *A. africanus*. A third one *A. boisei*, is added by some scientists. The species earlier referred to as *Homo habilis* is considered by some scientists to be more properly designated *A. habilis*, i.e. related to *Australopithecus* more closely than to *Homo*.

The family tree of the hominids, as known so far, probably appears as shown in Fig. 1 below.

Figure 1: *Probable Family Tree of the Hominids from* Ramapithecus *to* Homo.

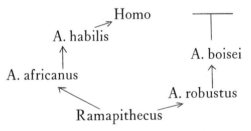

It will be seen from this figure that *Homo* is considered to have evolved through the lineage *A. africanus* and *A.*

habilis whilst the other, through *A. robustus* and *A. boisei*, was to end in extinction, perhaps about 1.5 million years ago.

What do we know about these two lineages of ape-men, and how did they differ from each other? Briefly, they differed in size, and their teeth suggest that they differed in dietary habits. This suggests differences in their ways of life. *A. africanus* was about the size of a modern chimpanzee, walked erect (although probably not entirely like we do) and may have eaten meat as well as fruit, roots and so on. In short, he was a hunter as well as a gatherer. *A. robustus* was taller, and bigger in body size than *A. africanus*, but his large powerful teeth suggest a vegetarian diet, requiring energetic chewing. *Australopithecus* had a brain of between 400 to 550 cubic centimeters, *robustus* and *boisei* being slightly bigger in this respect than *africanus*, and *habilis* exceeding all three with a brain size rising to a maximum of almost 650 c.c. Finds of stone tools at many sites bear witness to the beginnings of a material culture, reflecting the daily activities of these earliest men.

The next stage in the evolution of man is represented by fossil finds of *Homo erectus*. Most of these finds were made in Asia, near Peking in China, and in Java, Indonesia. Similar finds have been made in Europe, and in North, East, and South Africa. The finds are dated to between 300,000 and 500,000 years ago. The main differences between *Australopithecus* and *Homo erectus* is in body size and stature and in the development of the brain. The cultural evidence associated with *H. erectus*, for example stone choppers and hand-axes, the use of fire, the occupation of caves, also reflect a large step forward in the evolutionary development of mankind. The brain size of *H. erectus* had increased to around 1000 c.c., or about twice that of *Australopithecus*, and about two-thirds of that of contemporary man. The numerous finds of *H. erectus* that have come to light look remarkably alike, and suggest that man was already becoming mobile and migratory as a species.

Figure 2: *Geographical Localities of Main Finds of Early Hominids with Approximate Chronological Ranges (millions of years).*

India ⎱	China? ⎱	China ⎱
	Java?	Java
Ramapithecus *Australo-pithecus*		Germany
		Homo Erectus Hungary?
		N. Africa
	E. Africa	E. Africa
E. Africa ⎰	S. Africa ⎰	S. Africa ⎰
?15.0 - 10.0	?5.0 - 1.0	? 1.0 - ? 0.05

Pliocene 2.0   *Pleistocene*

It is difficult to say precisely where and when *H. erectus* was replaced by a more advanced species. There was probably a considerable overlap in time periods before one was replaced entirely by the other. Finds at Temara (Morocco), Mughharet-el-Aliya (Tangier) and Haua Fteah (Libya) suggest that isolated *"erectus*-like" people may have survived in North Africa until about 40,000 years ago.

Evidence from about 200,000 years ago, on the other hand, gives us a clear indication of man's next significant step in evolutionary progress—the emergence of *Homo sapiens*, the immediate forerunner of modern man, and the species that was to evolve and diversify sub-specifically into the major divisions of living mankind.

At Swanscombe (England) and Steinheim (Germany), finds have been made of practically complete skulls that contained brains of about 1200 c.c. in size. This figure lies within the range for living man. Further, cranial finds of similar brain size, and dated to between 70,000 and 100,000 years ago have been made at Ehringsdorf (Germany), Saccopastore (Italy), and Fontechevade (France). A find at Vertesszöllös (Hungary) is especially interesting as it may predate all other *H. sapiens* finds so far known. Outside Europe, finds of early *H. sapiens* have been made at Omo (Ethiopia) and Kanjera (Kenya), dating from about 90,000 to 100,000 years ago.

As we approach more recent times in prehistory, so the numbers of finds of *H. sapiens* grow more numerous and more widespread in their geographical distribution. Dating between about 75,000 and 45,000 years ago a distinctive population of *Homo sapiens* has left its skeletal and cultural traces in many parts of the world. So distinctive is this population that it has been given sub-specific status within *H. sapiens* to distinguish it from "men-like-us" who were to follow close on their heels.

A great deal has been written about *H. sapiens neandertalensis*, or Neandertal Man, because of the many finds that have been made and the intriguing problems that his prehistory presents (particularly his apparent disappearance eventually from the human evolutionary scene). The original find after which the group was named was made in the Neander Valley of Germany. Western Europe yielded many other remains that in physical appearance appeared to form a very homogeneous group and look somewhat different from Neandertaloid finds in other parts of Europe and in Africa and Asia. Resemblances to earlier *Homo sapiens* finds (Swanscombe Man and Steinheim Man) are also obvious. One plausible explanation of the distinctiveness of the "classic" Western European Neandertals is that they were cut off from other contemporary populations by the ice sheets and glaciers that covered parts of Europe in those times. They made fine stone tools, were great hunters, and buried their dead with appropriate ceremonials. Their brains were of the size of those of modern man or, in some cases, even larger, as indicated by cranial capacity.

Evidence from farther east in Europe and from areas such as Israel, Lebanon and Iraq suggest the appearance about 45,000 and 55,000 years ago of men who were intermediate in appearance between the Western European Neandertals and modern man. Migrants who were fully evolved modern men arrived in Western and Central Europe about 40,000 years ago, coming apparently from

Eastern Europe, North Africa and Western Asia, with new tool-making traditions that appear to have abruptly replaced those of their Neandertal predecessors.

The overall picture at this time period is of a mosaic of peoples ranging from those retaining Neandertaloid resemblances to peoples virtually indistinguishable skeletally from many contemporary populations of man. The differentiation of *Homo sapiens* had truly begun.

THE EARLIEST SKELETAL EVIDENCE OF TODAY'S "RACES"

There are by now almost 200 archaeological sites that have yielded remains of fossil man that can be dated with reasonable accuracy to the Neolithic or New Stone Age in Europe. They lived between about 35,000 and 10,000 years ago and from the appearance of their skulls and other bones, supplemented by numerous measurements, it is clear that they differed little from many of the present-day peoples of Europe.

One of the best-known of these early European finds is that of Cro-Magnon Man near Les Eyzies in France. The Cro-Magnon site yielded skeletal remains and stone implements buried in a cave. Examination of this and many other sites has revealed that the peoples named after Cro-Magnon Man were a tall, well-built people with large heads and eye-sockets and wide faces. Their chins and nasal bridges were well-developed. When compared with mankind today they most nearly resemble (in skeletal features) modern Europeans such as the Scandinavians, British of the "Anglo-Saxon" type and the Irish. We know nothing, of course, of their skin, hair or eye colour, or of their facial features and hair type.

Many of these early Europeans were prolific artists, carving bone, antler, ivory and limestone, and also engraving and painting. More animals are depicted than men, but there are some realistic representations of the latter. Men are shown bearded, sometimes bald and usually with prominent noses. Statues and bas-reliefs of women show them as abnormally obese, but some of this may be deliberate distortion. Cro-Magnon Man had a brain size equal to that of modern Europeans, and had a rich material culture. Adapting many of the tool-making techniques of the earlier Neandertals, he refined the processes of working with stone and bone. With his spears, knives and slings, and his traps, enclosures and pitfalls, he was a skilful hunter, often using the techniques of ambush and stampede to make large-scale killings, much as Canada's Indians and Eskimos were to hunt the bison and caribou in early times. The nature of the art of Cro-Magnon Man, and the caves where he practised it, suggest the beginnings of magic, ritual and ceremonial and therefore the origins of religion.

Neolithic Europeans were spread throughout Western and Eastern Europe. Some of the most easterly-located representatives come from the cave of Hotu in Iran, and look very similar to their western contemporaries. Descendants of these easterners were to migrate into North Africa, and the ones who stayed behind in Western Asia were to be the first people to grow crops and to domesticate some of the animals of those times. These agricultural activities were accompanied by new stone-making techniques—the Neolithic or New Stone Age—and were to form the basis of later civilizations.

The skeletons found in North Africa that are somewhat similar to the early Europeans of Western Asia have already been mentioned. Whilst there are some differences, mainly heavier brow-ridges and wider skulls and noses that distinguish these early Africans, there is nothing that can be considered particularly Negroid about them. Skeletal remains of about fifty of these strongly-built people have been discovered at Afalou-bou-Rhummel; they are estimated to have lived there about 10,000 years ago.

At Singa, in the Sudan, partial remains of a skull about 20,000 years old show the narrow projecting forehead common to many Negroid peoples today. Similar finds have been made in East Africa, dated to about 10,000 years ago.

The most typically Negroid find, however, comes from Asselar in Mali (Southern Sahara), where an almost complete skeleton has been dated to 6,000 years ago and exhibits most of the characteristics of modern African Negroids, particularly the Bantu.

The Hottentots and Bushmen of Southern Africa are much shorter in stature than other Negroids, although now generally considered to be related to them. A reduction in body size is thought to have begun about 8,000 or 9,000 years ago, but the reasons for this still elude us.

If we turn to Asia and review the bones that show resemblances to those of contemporary man we find that both the Mongoloid and the Australoid peoples are represented.

Discoveries of human remains from late Palaeolithic times have been made in China and Japan, and excavations are continuing. At Chou-kou-tien, near Peking, the so-called Upper Cave has yielded remains of individuals that show skeletal signs of Mongoloid characteristics. Some investigators have been struck by resemblances between these strongly-featured people and skeletal remains of early American Indians. They may represent, therefore, an "early-Mongoloid" or "archaic-Mongoloid" stock, that was eventually to be replaced in Eastern Asia by "late-Mongoloid" or "recent-Mongoloid" peoples such as the present-day Chinese. In North America, representatives of such recent Mongoloids would be the Eskimo, who arrived perhaps no more than 5,000 years ago from Siberia, and slowly moved eastward across the Arctic. Finds from Tze-Yung (Szechuan) and Liu-Kiang (Kwangsi) in China and from near Mikkabi (Japan) also point to the emergence of early Mongoloids, but dating can only be broadly suggested as Upper Pleistocene.

In the Solo River valley (Central Java) remains of early man have been found, dated perhaps about 100,000 to 65,000 years ago that show resemblances to both *Homo erectus* in Java and to later *Homo sapiens* in South-east Asia. Solo Man is sometimes called an Asian Neandertal.

If his skulls are placed in line with those from Wadjak (Java), Niah (Borneo) and the earliest from Australia itself, there appears to be an obvious evolutionary progression ending in an Austroloid type. The Niah Cave find has been reliably dated to 40,000 years ago. This evidence seems to indicate where Australoids may have evolved and their subsequent migratory progress, entering Australia perhaps 12,000 years ago.

The skeletal documentation of the earliest American arrival is still not clear. Archaeological evidence suggests man entered America at least 30,000 years ago and moved southwards, using the ice-free corridor that existed east of the Rocky Mountains from Alaska to the area of the Great Plains. Unique types of tools found in Arizona show that American man was hunting mastodon there at least 10,000 years ago. Campsites in Argentina and southern Chile have been dated to 8,000 years ago, showing how rapidly man penetrated his New World.

The skeletal evidence of all this is not extensive, as yet. Finds have been made at Punin in Ecuador, Pelican Rapids, Minnesota, Tepexpan in Mexico and Midland, Texas. The Mexican find is about 11,000 years old and the Texan find about 8,700 years. All these skeletal finds look much like modern American Indians.

A recent new find in Canada is of considerable interest. Portions of a crushed skull including some teeth have been recovered from Tabor Hill, Alberta, and the geological evidence has been tentatively interpreted as indicating an antiquity of between 30,000 and 60,000 years. The remains are that of a baby and it is difficult to say more than that it appears clearly to be *Homo sapiens*. The earliest human remains so far discovered in Arctic Canada resemble modern Eskimos and are about 2,500 years old.

We have reviewed, very briefly, some of the skeletal evidence for the differentiation of *Homo sapiens* and shown what we know of some of his migrations. An attempt has been made to show the beginnings of sub-specific skeletal variation. The fossil evidence seems to show that as man evolved, he moved from tropical Africa through latitudes characterized by many different climates and geographical environments.

Today the majority of physical anthropologists and human biologists are convinced that many differences in human aspects such as behaviour, culture, physiological function, body proportions and appearance are the results of adaptation to these different environments. We learn nothing of many of these aspects when we examine the bones of our most recent ancestors. But a study of living man, particularly of populations that have remained in one area for long periods of time, suggests that of such adaptations many of the physical ones, such as skin colour, are capable of being "fixed" genetically through the course of time, although this does not preclude, in any way, the possibility of further subsequent changes.

We shall look next, then, at what we know of human adaptability today, its genetic determinants, and their interaction with man's different environments.

Chapter 3

Inheritance, Environment and Human Adaptability

Mention has already been made of the importance of genetics, particularly human genetics, to the study of mankind and to the understanding of the principles underlying human variability.

Today, these principles are known to many people especially those concerned with the breeding of plants and animals. A rose gardener or a wheat farmer knows well what qualities he wishes to find and perpetuate in his plants, and utilizes the science of genetics accordingly. The dog-breeder or racehorse-breeder works with the same basic premises. Thus, roses can be bred to bloom with a certain colour; wheat can be bred to give a high yield or a disease-resistant strain; dogs can be bred to produce distinctive coats of hair or other characters, and horses can be bred for speed and stamina or, if necessary, for brute strength. Similarly, cows can be bred to be good milk-yielders, pigs to produce a high meat return, and hens to be prolific egg-layers.

It is hardly surprising, then, that the same basic genetic principles that apply to these plants and animals can be applied to man himself. It matters not whether the observed variation is naturally or artificially induced; the principles are the same. Thus, when we see a "pedigree" poodle, or bulldog or Doberman pinscher, or a Jersey or Holstein cow, we find no difficulty in recognizing that there are traits or characteristics that set such animals apart from other dogs or other cows, and apart from each other, within their respective groups. These domestic breeds can be considered as rigidly differentiated races, so long as hybridization with other breeds is not allowed to occur. If we look more widely at the world of nature, we soon realize however that natural races occur everywhere. There are differences, small or large, between, say, sparrows, crabs, elephants, camels, squirrels and so on, found in different parts of a continent or in different parts of the world. The main difference between "natural" races of such animals and the "artificial" races of the animal-breeder, is that the former tend to merge into one another in terms of characteristics rather than to display the clear-cut discrete distinctions that have been deliberately encouraged in the latter by man.

Our knowledge today of how such variation comes about is drawn from the findings of many scientists working in many disciplines. We can single out, however, the work of two pioneers for special mention. One is the abbott Gregor Mendel, who first suggested the laws of heredity in 1806, following breeding experiments with peas and other plants in his monastery garden; the other is Charles Darwin who, unaware of Mendel's work, found a wide (if initially sceptical) audience for his writings on evolution, natural selection and the "survival of the fittest" after 1859 when he published his great work *On the Origin of the Species by Means of Natural Selection*.

Another important finding was emphasized in 1839 by two Germans, Schleiden and Schwann, who elaborated on Robert Hooke's earlier observation in 1665 that all living things are made up of cells. The emerging science of genetics was to show that within these cells lay the secrets of reproduction and evolutionary progress.

Today, then, if we look at the components of the human body, say, muscle, hair, nerve or bone, we find cells present. They may vary in overall shape, but have structural similarities. Each cell is contained within an outer cellular membrane. Within this membrane is a substance called cytoplasm. This surrounds a denser nucleus divided from the cytoplasm by another membrane. Within the nucleus lie a number of rod-like chromosomes which carry units of heritable material called genes. The composition of a cell is shown in a generalized diagrammatic form in Figure 3.

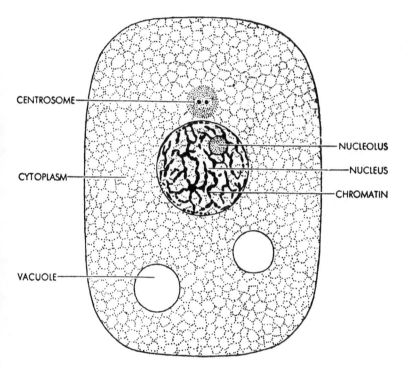

Figure 3: Diagrammatic representation of a cell and some of its parts.

Using the analogy of the computer, and the punch-card or tape programme that supplies it with its operating instructions, we can regard genes or groups of genes as programming the development in the human body of such characteristics as skin, hair and eye pigmentation, the shape of ears, noses and lips, and so on. Much remains to be learned about human genes; we do not even know how many one cell nucleus or one chromosome contains. Estimates have ranged up to and beyond 100,000 genes in each of man's cells, even as many as one million genes! Simple organic structures such as viruses contain perhaps ten genes, but the more complex the structure is, the more complex its genetic programme must be, and the more numerous will be its genes (Stern, 1960).

Putting it very simply, genes are now known to be made up of a complicated chemical called deoxyribonucleic acid, or DNA. DNA can vary in its precise makeup, and thus different genes have different chemical components, in the same way as the sentences on this page might contain different words, but still all be sentences of this book. Upon occasion, the DNA of a gene may undergo a spontaneous change in its makeup. When this change occurs, it is known as mutation, and enables new variation to arise in an organism, by effectively changing the genetic programming. Some causes of mutation will be discussed later.

As might be expected, if the number of genes can vary from one organism to another, so the complement of chromosomes will also have varied. Man has 23 pairs of chromosomes within his cellular nuclei, and these pairs can be identified under the microscope, using special techniques. One set of these chromosomes is inherited from an individual's male parent and the other set from the female parent. Each child, then, in its genetic makeup, is a cross between its father and its mother. The genetic makeup, unique to each and every individual, is referred to as the "genotype". The assembly of genotypes existing within a human population may be referred to as its gene pool—a term we have already encountered. Assuming that a population is reproducing itself by endogamy or inbreeding only, then the only source of new variation within the community (except for new combinations or permutations of genes) will be mutation. However, the composition of a gene pool in such a population can slowly change in time, for it is the genotypes of the breeders in a population that will be the basis of gene pools of subsequent generations. Exogamy, or out-breeding, on the other hand, may introduce atypical genes into a population.

One of the 23 pairs of human chromosomes is that involved in determining the sex of each individual. Sex chromosomes are of two kinds, designated X and Y. The female has two X chromosomes whilst the male has one X and one Y. When parents each pass on their one set of chromosomes to their offspring the possibilities of sex determination are as shown in Figure 4.

Figure 4: Situation A

MOTHER		FATHER
XX	SEX CHROMOSOMES	XY

| EGG X | | X SPERM |

FERTILIZATION

XX

DAUGHTER

Situation B

MOTHER		FATHER
XX	SEX CHROMOSOMES	XY

| EGG X | | Y SPERM |

FERTILIZATION

XY

SON

The mechanism of sex determination, therefore, provides for the permutation of chromosomes and genes and ensures that each child, whilst genetically similar to both its parents, is genetically identical with neither of them. In a sense, each child is a hybrid of its parents, who in turn are hybrids of their parents.

It must be emphasized next that although the effects of possessing a certain genotype may be apparent in any individual (say, in his skin colour, or in the possession of a distinctively-shaped nose or chin), the genotype itself remains concealed and can only be determined for those characters (such as certain of the blood groups) whose mode of inheritance is fairly simple and susceptible to genetic analysis. We do not know precisely how many gene pairs are responsible for determining a person's skin colour or hair colour, for example, although we may readily observe by inspection that they are dark brown. What we are inspecting, then, is referred to as the phenotype. A further complication is that some phenotypes may be modified by environmental influences. Thus a man may be tall because his parents were tall, or because although born to parents of medium height, his nutrition, exercise and activity patterns may have enabled him to surpass the height of his parents. Although the genetic potential for tallness might have existed in the parents, their way of life might have precluded their full realization of this potential.

The distinction between phenotype and genotype can be readily understood by reference to the mode of inheritance of the well-known ABO blood group system. This system is common to all mankind (and certain of its primate relatives) and manifests itself by the presence or absence of certain substances called antigens in the red blood corpuscles or cells. These antigens are A and B, O denoting their complete absence. Some people's red corpuscles carry both A and B antigen, giving them a blood group AB. These four blood groups, easily identifiable by serological tests, are the ABO phenotypes, and the fact of belonging to any one group is determined by one pair of genes or alleles. Of these genes (which will be underlined

to distinguish them from the antigens) A and B are of
equal expressive power or co-dominant, whilst both A
and B are dominant over O. The possible phenotypes and
genotypes in this blood group system therefore are as
follows:

ABO Blood Group System

Phenotype	Antigen Present	Possible Genotype
A	A	AA or AO
B	B	BB or BO
AB	A and B	AB
O	none	OO

You will see that in the cases of phenotype AB and O
it is possible to say precisely what the genotype is, as only
one can be present in each case. In the case of phenotype
A and B, however, we can only say that the genotype *must*
contain A and B respectively, but we have no direct
method of ascertaining which other genes are present. If
we know the parental phenotypes, it is possible sometimes
to be certain of the genotypes of their offspring. Some
examples follow:

	Father	Mother		Father	Mother
phenotype	O	AB	phenotype	AB	AB
genotype	OO	AB	genotype	AB	AB
	Child 1	Child 2		Child 1	Child 2
phenotype	B	A	phenotype	A	B
genotype	BO	AO	genotype	AA	BB

	Father	Mother		Father	Mother
phenotype	A	AB	phenotype	A	O
genotype	AA	AB	genotype	AA or AO	OO
	Child 1	Child 2		Child 1	Child 2
phenotype	A	AB	phenotype	A	O
genotype	AA	AB	genotype	AO	OO

Suppose that we look next at three rooms containing small groups of people, and let us suppose conventional blood tests show the following startling phenotypic results:

Room 1	Room 2	Room 3
A A A A A	A A A A A	A A A A A
A A A A A	A A A A A	A A A A A

but let us suppose the actual genotypic details to be as follows:

Room 1	Room 2	Room 3
$\underline{AA}$ $\underline{AA}$ $\underline{AA}$ $\underline{AO}$ $\underline{AO}$	$\underline{AO}$ $\underline{AA}$ $\underline{AO}$ $\underline{AA}$ $\underline{AO}$	$\underline{AO}$ $\underline{AA}$ $\underline{AO}$ $\underline{AO}$ $\underline{AA}$
$\underline{AA}$ $\underline{AO}$ $\underline{AA}$ $\underline{AA}$ $\underline{AA}$	$\underline{AO}$ $\underline{AA}$ $\underline{AA}$ $\underline{AA}$ $\underline{AO}$	$\underline{AO}$ $\underline{AO}$ $\underline{AO}$ $\underline{AO}$ $\underline{AO}$

Thus, although all three rooms contain people who are, upon testing, all found to be of blood group A, the gene frequencies of our three samples in fact differ very markedly. By counting the genes involved (always supposing that we were able to obtain the genotypic information) the frequencies of the actual genes responsible would be found to be as follows:

Gene Frequency of	Room 1	Room 2
$\underline{A}$ (p)	17/20 = 85% or 0.85	15/20 = 75% or 0.75
$\underline{B}$ (q)	0/20 = 0% or 0.00	0/20 = 0% or 0.00
$\underline{O}$ (r)	3/20 = 15% or 0.15	5/20 = 25% or 0.25

Gene Frequency of	Room 3
A (p)	12/20 = 60% or 0.60
B (q)	0/20 = 0% or 0.00
O (r)	8/20 = 40% or 0.40

(The symbols p, q and r are used to indicate the *frequencies* of genes $\underline{A}$ $\underline{B}$ and $\underline{O}$ respectively.)

Blood-group gene frequencies cannot always be counted in this simple fashion, so that resort has to be made to mathematical formulae to obtain the necessary data after the blood-group tests have been made. Such data are often referred to as genetic markers, and can give guidance as to affinities between populations and even to suggest possible migration routes.

For example, certain Indian tribes in northern and western Canada (and in Alaska) have a frequency of blood group A of between 10 per cent and 19 per cent. Investigation shows that these Indians speak dialects of the Athabaskan linguistic division. Looking elsewhere amongst American Indians for Athabaskan speakers, we find the Navajo and Apache in the Southwest of the U.S.A. They also have a group A frequency of between 10 per cent and 19 per cent whilst their Indian neighbours fall between 1 per cent and 9 per cent. The findings are supported by what we know of the migratory movements of the Apache and Navajo—they arrived in the southwest U.S.A. only a few hundred years ago, recently enough for little or no change in their group A frequency to have taken place by intermarriage and hybridization with other peoples.

So far as we know, a person's blood groups are unaffected by his external environment and thus remain unchanged throughout his life. But, as has been mentioned before, many other human characteristics such as stature or body build are only partially determined by heredity, and may be modified by environment. We must distinguish too between hereditary adaptation in man (the dark skin of the Negroid, for example) and acquired adaptation (the dark skin of a heavily sun-tanned European).

Before turning to a study of human adaptability (which attempts to explain *why* there may be these phenotypic and genotypic differences between peoples) let us look briefly at a few more genetic markers that appear to distinguish certain populations from others.

Blood is only one aspect of the internal chemistry of the human body. Urine is another. It is common knowledge that analysis of human urine may reveal evidence of diabetes—a disease preventing the body from properly disposing of sugar. Many other chemical variations are detectable by analysis of urine. A substance known as beta-amino-isobutyric acid (BAIB) is excreted in large amounts in the urine of Asians, such as Chinese, and of related Mongoloids, such as groups of Amerindians. Excretion of BAIB is much lower in most European populations, however. Comparison of BAIB excretion in a sample of Negroes and Europeans has revealed differences even though they were living together and consuming the same diet, thus emphasizing the genetic aspect of the variation and excluding environmental factors.

A chemical known as phenyl-thiocarbamide (PTC) tastes bitter to some people, but is tasteless to others. Investigation has shown that this difference in ability to taste PTC is genetically controlled. Moreover, human populations differ in the frequency of tasters and non-tasters. About 30 per cent of Australian aborigines are tasters, whilst about 70 per cent of African Negroes and 85 to 90 per cent of Amerindians can taste the substance. However, what this difference means is something that we are as yet unable to explain, as is also the case in BAIB excretion patterns.

Albinism (lack of pigmentation in skin, hair and eyes) appears to be caused by the body's failure to produce melanin, the pigment essential for normal skin, hair and eye colour. Such failure is believed to happen through an enzyme deficiency. The frequency of albinism varies from population to population, but is seldom noticeably high. One of the highest incidences is found in the San Blas Indians of Panama where a phenotypic frequency of .007 (seven tenths of 1 per cent) has been recorded, a figure about 150 times as high as that reported for Europeans. Albinism is noticeable in Hopi Indians, and is also found in Japan, Melanesia and Africa.

A number of vision defects is included in the term colour-blindness. Differences in the perception of shades of green seem to vary considerably between populations. It is suggested that colour-blindness is almost absent in Amerindians and Pacific peoples, and very low in African Negroes, in contrast to peoples in other parts of the world. Human cerumen, or earwax, occurs in two kinds— "sticky" and "dry". This appears to be genetically controlled and thus can be used as a marker. About 85 per cent of Japanese have a dry, flaky type of earwax. This type is also the more common type in other Mongoloids such as the Navajo (60 to 70 per cent) and the Sioux and Dakota Amerindians (45 to 55 per cent). Negroes and Europeans have lower frequencies, i.e. sticky earwax is more commonly observed.

It is common knowledge that no two individuals have identical fingerprints. Prints can be described and classified in many ways but the simplest division is into arches, loops and whorls. The numbers of these can be counted in individuals and also in samples of populations. Family studies show that these features are heritable, and we know that they cannot be changed by environment. Peoples in Europe and Africa typically have high loop frequencies and low whorl frequencies. In India and the Near East, frequencies are reversed, loops being low and whorls being high. In Asia and North America, frequencies of loops and whorls resemble each other fairly closely. Arches are usually low in frequency in world populations except in African pygmies and Bushmen in whom they rise to 10 per cent or over.

Population or race differences can be seen to occur throughout the body, internally and externally, and involve many features less obvious than some of those already quoted. There are differences in limb proportions, muscles, distribution patterns of subcutaneous fat, teeth, degrees of metabolic activity, and so on. Some of these differences are so obvious that they seem even to preclude any overlapping between populations. For example, the spiral-tufted hair of the African Bushman or Hottentot (which also occurs in some Andamanese Islanders) can be said to be completely absent in Europeans. Within the Rhesus blood-group system, the Rhesus-negative gene is virtually absent everywhere, except within Europe and emigrant Caucasoid populations.

Many other traits, however, are so widespread that they have given rise to misunderstandings regarding affinities between human populations. Thus the dark skin pigmentation of the African Negro and the Melanesian of New Guinea implies no close genetic connection, any more than does the fact that an individual Englishman, Chinese or Negro might all be of blood group B within the ABO system.

We may, then, if we wish, regard a race as an endogamous or inbreeding population, large or small, that has come through time to be characterized by gene frequencies that are different from those of other populations. But when such a race resorts for one reason or another to exogamy or out-breeding, these gene frequencies will begin to change, and the earlier genetic identity of the population will be lost. A new genetic identity is being formed. Some reason for this might be migration (in response to food shortages or to escape aggression), local shortages of marriageable partners (perhaps through disease, catastrophe or warfare), and so on.

Let us look next at the value to man of some of these distinctive characteristics. An examination of a world map of the skin colour of mankind, for example, shows a clear pattern of distribution. Generally speaking, dark-skinned peoples live in hot and low latitudes, light-skinned people live in cooler and higher ones. What is the significance of this and other apparent instances of man's adaptability to his environment?

A very obvious feature of man's natural environment, and one that is brought daily to his attention is the amount and degree of solar radiation to which he is exposed. Solar radiation varies with latitude, equatorial latitudes experiencing the most.

When man is exposed to sunshine, he is exposed to heat, via infra-red rays, and possibly to skin trauma (suntan to sunburn, even to skin cancer) via the ultra-violet rays.

The amount of solar radiation that an individual absorbs

may have important influences upon his comfort, health and nutritional status. Skin colour provides one natural way of regulating the amount of solar radiation that may be absorbed.

Skin colour, together with hair and eye colour, is principally determined by the presence of a chemical pigment called melanin. It is the density and distribution of melanin, then, that determines an individual's "basic" skin colour (remembering that this may be temporarily darkened in some people by sun-tanning).

First of all, then, a dark skin colour appears to offer some protection against the effects of the amounts of solar radiation experienced in tropical latitudes. Lightly-pigmented Europeans are at a disadvantage in such conditions. Many do not possess the ability to tan readily, and thus must avoid exposure to sunlight as much as possible.

However, a dark skin, whilst reflecting (i.e. "turning back") ultra-violet rays, also absorbs more heat from infra-red rays than does a light skin. This, in turn, may raise the body's internal temperature quickly to the sweating point, thus assisting the cooling process that then takes place through evaporation of perspiration.

Tanning ability varies from people to people. It may be especially useful in latitudes where the sunlight might be bright, but high temperatures are not encountered on a year-round basis. Canada's Eskimos (or Inuit), for example, have a yellow-brown skin colour, but the exposed parts of the body (mainly face and hands) of hunters may tan to a very dark colour during the long summer days of sunshine.

There is also a connection between vitamin D, responsible for calcium metabolism, and solar radiation. Inadequate vitamin D results in insufficient calcium, and bones may be affected. Rickets, with bowing of the legs and spinal deformation, is a well-known calcium deficiency disease. On the other hand, an excess of vitamin D may result in over-deposition of calcium with brittle, easily fractured bones and deposition of nodules in parts of the body such as the kidneys.

With the exception of oil from the livers of the codfish and halibut, most foodstuffs contain little or no vitamin D. Upon exposure to the sun's ultra-violet rays, however, a layer of cells immediately beneath the skin has the ability to synthesize vitamin D. For this to happen the rays must penetrate the skin (and its melanin screen) in order to reach the underlying cells.

The minimum daily requirement of vitamin D has been estimated at 400 units. It is suggested that an area of "white" skin about the size of the cheeks, exposed to sunlight in temperate latitudes during the day, is capable of permitting the synthesis of this amount. A much larger area of "black" skin would have to be exposed under the same circumstances, and even then might not result in the minimum daily vitamin D requirement being reached. In the tropics, on the other hand, the amount of ultra-violet radiation striking the "black" skin would be considerably higher and would offer no hindrance to adequate vitamin D synthesis.

Skeletal evidence suggests that man evolved in the tropics. Thus, early man was probably darkly pigmented. As his subsequent migrations led him away from such latitudes, so he came to occupy lands where solar radiation was less intense. As at that period he had little in the way of complex cultural adaptation (for example, cod-liver oil, vitamin D enriched milk or calcium tablets) to affect his adjustment, adaptation to such new environmental conditions would have had to be physiological in nature. Man may well have gone through at this time a selection process favouring lighter pigmentation in terms of survival value. If we discount the greater mobility and cultural advantages of more recent man, the world distribution of pigmentation seems to bear this out.

Heat has already been mentioned as an environmental stress affecting man, and there are other ways in which man has adapted to exposure to it besides dark pigmentation. The purpose of such adaptations appears to be to dissipate heat as efficiently as possible. Heat flows from hot to cold, so body heat is transferred through the skin, and especially through the body's extremities. An elongated lean body, with long arms and legs, therefore, is an ideal body build to lose body heat. It provides more surface area relative to the body mass than a stockier build. Many African people tend to be somewhat tall, with long arms and legs, as do some of the peoples of Melanesia. There are disconcerting exceptions, of course, such as the pygmies of equatorial Africa and South-east Asia.

Experiments carried out on U.S. soldiers moving in a hot humid environment have shown that Blacks and Whites (selected so as to be of similar weight and with similar acclimatization) differ in response, the Black maintaining a lower internal temperature. This finding suggests genetic differences in heat tolerance. One would suppose, therefore, that Blacks, when exposed to cold, would not fare as well as Whites. Evidence from winters during the Korean War shows that Black soldiers suffered a higher incidence of cold-related injuries than did their white compatriots.

In regions such as the Arctic, where the cold is a primary stress, a stocky thickset body, with relatively short extremities, serves to conserve internal body heat. The Eskimo has this kind of physique, but we should remember that without many cultural adaptations (warm, light clothing; fire; snow houses) he could not have survived the rigours of the circumpolar region. In fact, the only parts of the Eskimo usually exposed to the cold are his face and hands; the remainder of his body, swathed in caribou skins and furs, may be exposed to virtually subtropical conditions.

Tests show that Eskimos have an inherent tolerance for cold greater than that of most other peoples. If his fingers are immersed in ice-water they remain warm, whilst those of other people immediately react to the cold. The basal metabolic rate is higher in Eskimos, and their central nervous system appears to be adapted to tolerate cold discomfort. Contrary to popular opinion, Eskimos are not a fat people. It is their build and their bulky clothing that make them look so.

There is evidence that a certain degree of cold tolerance can be acquired through repeated exposure to cold. Canadian fishermen of the Maritimes, for example, become gradually acclimatized to working with their hands in icy cold water and can put up with discomfort that other people would find quite unbearable.

This has been explained by a process of habituation of the nervous system to cold. The fact that older fishermen in Canada's Maritime provinces lose this tolerance after retirement from the sea bears out the suggestion that acclimatization rather than adaptation is responsible.

If we look at the world's populations as a whole, a clear relationship appears to be demonstrated between average body weight and prevailing climate. The British human biologist D. F. Roberts has shown that populations where the average adult male body weight is over 130 lbs are almost always found in temperate and cold regions and hardly ever in the tropics. The exceptions are usually migrant populations who have not occupied a particular area long enough for this kind of body adaptation to have taken place.

Another instance of adaptation to cold has been noted in the Australian aboriginal who sleeps out in the open practically naked, at winter temperatures of around 37° F. Upon investigation it has been found the aborigine has the physiological ability to allow his body surface temperature to drop slowly during the night whilst his internal core temperature remains constant, and his metabolic rate remains low. A European, on the other hand, lacking this adaptation, would react by means of an elevated metabolic rate, burning off more and more calories in an effort to generate enough heat to keep his body surface temperature from dropping lower as the night goes on.

Few other human physical characteristics have such a clearly demonstrated adaptive value. The study of human adaptability is still in its infancy, and although we can record much of what we see of human variation we can, as yet, seldom explain its significance. Hair type, body hair patterns, eye, ear and lip shape, facial proportions, and so on, are some examples. We have broad-headed peoples and long-headed peoples, wide-faced peoples and narrow-faced peoples, and such distinctions are not confined to any one population. A reasonably convincing argument for adaptation in at least one facial feature can be made. This is an apparent association between nose shape, as expressed by an index, and climate. The maximum breadth of the nose is divided by its length giving a nasal index. The wider the nose, the higher this index will be, and this wide nasal shape is more common in peoples living in hot humid climates. In Africa, for example, such peoples have an average index of 76 to 105, and their climate has a mean annual temperature of 70° F to 83° F, with a mean annual humidity of 71 to 90 per cent. By contrast, Africans living in hot, dry climates have a mean nasal index of 65 to 87, living in average temperatures of 70° F to 84° F and average humidity of 33 to 52 per cent. Similar differences in nasal index can be found in different climatic zones of Asia and America.

If we compare measurements of climatic humidity and nasal indices by statistical means we obtain a significantly high correlation of +0.82 (an absolute positive correlation would be +1.0), and the correlation between mean climatic temperature and nasal index is +0.63.

The adaptations so far discussed have come about in response to stresses of various kinds, such as heat, humidity, cold, and solar radiation. Disease is another important stress that has acted upon human populations.

The opening up of Canada's North has been accompanied by tragic evidence of differences in man's resistance to disease.

In the late 1940's, military exercises were held by Canadian armed forces in the Fort Chimo area. Eskimos with their dog teams were recruited to help in the manoeuvres. After they were over, the Eskimos dispersed once more to their hunting camps near George River and Payne Bay. Unfortunately, a case of measles had been introduced from the south and the disease spread rapidly through the camps. Before messages had been received by the medical authorities, and help flown in, about a third of the Eskimo population in the affected camps had died.

In the early 1950's, an Eskimo in Churchill, Manitoba, came into contact with poliomyelitis. He returned to his home at Eskimo Point, and from there another Eskimo travelled to Padlei and a Roman Catholic priest travelled to Chesterfield Inlet. Soon, poliomyelitis broke out in both settlements. At Chesterfield, some 85 per cent of the population was stricken, a third of the sufferers dying or becoming severely paralyzed.

In 1962, an epidemic of tuberculosis occurred in Eskimo Point. Beginning with a single case, some ninety inhabitants eventually required hospital treatment out of a total population of some three hundred Eskimos.

Indian populations, both in Canada and elsewhere in North America, have from time to time been severely affected by diseases such as measles, scarlet fever and small pox. Such epidemics were particularly virulent when the first European invaders began to push across the continent. In the Old World, measles and scarlet fever had been known for centuries and, although responsible for deaths, had virtually been relegated to the status of "childhood diseases", usually quickly thrown off and non-lethal. European populations had apparently become resistant to these diseases through natural selection, generation after generation, and even more serious epidemics such as small pox did not kill off everybody in an afflicted population. When the responsible bacteria and viruses reached the New World, however, devastating results occurred in encounters with the non-resistant indigenous peoples. Whole tribes, for example the Mandan Indians of the Great Plains, were virtually wiped out by disease in a matter of weeks. Eventually, of course, cultural adaptation (drugs and medical care) was to eliminate the severity of most of these hazards to health, but even today tuberculosis and other respiratory ailments remain potentially or actually dangerous to many of Canada's northern peoples.

We must remember, though, that prior to the arrival of Europeans in Canada, the Indians and Eskimos were just as "fit" as the Europeans had been in the Old World; they simply had not previously come into contact with the diseases that were then introduced. Our knowledge of human origins, differentiation and distribution is inextricably mixed with what we know of the history and geography of disease. Differences in customs and ways of life have always been significant. The high incidence of tuberculosis in Canadian Indians and Métis by contrast to other Canadians reflects in part their comparative poverty with inadequate or imbalanced nutrition, sub-standard housing with crowded living conditions, and so on. Vaccination and innoculation alone are insufficient to eradicate some of the diseases.

It is now thought that as dietary habits and food levels, use of alcohol and tobacco, patterns of daily and seasonal activity, customary age of first intercourse and marriage, social custom and preference in marriage, number of children, interval between births, infant nursing practices, sanitary and contraceptive practices, may vary quite considerably from one population group to another, then such factors may well influence differences in fertility, morbidity and mortality that certainly appear.

Chapter 4

Race and Intelligence

There has long been speculation—most of it emotional and uninformed—regarding a possible connection between the brain size of man and his intelligence. There are, of course, some obvious correlations. We have seen how, as man evolved, so his cranial capacity increased, the australopithecines having a brain size averaging about 500 c.c., the pithecanthropines (*H. erectus*) about 980 c.c., and modern man about 1300 c.c., with a range between about 1000 c.c., and 2000 c.c. There is a clear progression until about 250,000 years ago, when *H. sapiens* emerged with a capacity within our modern range.

Similarly, our brains today are larger than those of any of our primate relatives, the highest cranial capacity recorded for any gorilla, for example, being about 750 c.c.

Brain size is a crude measurement, at best, being usually estimated from the cubic capacity of the braincase. Primate brains differ not only in gross size but in their complexity and development, and in their relation to body size.

So, although the larger a primate may be, the larger his brain will be (there will, of course, be exceptions), direct comparison will still be difficult. Gorilla brains and chimpanzee brains can be of similar magnitude, but it does not follow that the two genera are similar in mental or intellectual capacity. The brains of modern men and women differ, on an average, by about 150 to 200 c.c. in capacity. This, again, does not imply sexual differences in intelligence or other abilities. Elephants have far larger brains than man, but are not necessarily more sagacious. Whales have even larger brains.

One of the distinctive features of man's brain is its extensively convoluted surface pattern. This patterning is far more complex than that of the apes. These convolutions permit the area of the brain's surface to be greatly expanded without the necessity of expanding its volume. It has been estimated that man's brain surface covers some 200 square inches or more, at least 50 per cent greater than the surface area of a smooth sphere of similar size.

Differences in the relative sizes of the different parts and lobes of the brain also mark off man from his primate relatives and from other animals. Thus, the frontal lobe is well-developed in man (giving him his near-vertical forehead), controlling such things as attention span and the screening of stimuli being received. Parts of the temporal and parietal lobes of the cerebellum (at the base of the brain) control articulate and meaningful speech, and so on.

Our experience of man's accomplishments leads us to believe that in terms of perception, intelligence, initiative, perseverance, and other attributes, he has far surpassed all other animals. These are all mental abilities almost uniquely human, and controversy has long existed whether such abilities are innate in all human beings and, if so, whether they are present in equal quantities.

One concern of early classifiers of mankind was that if the world's peoples could be separated into clear racial divisions, then it would be an easy matter to measure one up against another in terms of intelligence and achievement, and thus draw up a hierarchy of "superior" and "inferior" races. Geographical and cultural isolation were widely recognized to haxe existed—could not men, therefore, have evolved differently in both physical and mental attributes? From this it was a short step to attempt to associate such attributes with each other. Put very simply, a common consensus was that "white" was considered superior to "black". "Yellow" lay somewhere in between.

Today, many psychologists have virtually abandoned the proposition that intelligence, however defined, can be accurately and objectively tested. Such tests as are now administered are usually done so with restricted objectives in mind and designed in accordance with the population sample being studied. A test devised for, say, Canadian Eskimos is unlikely to be as appropriate for testing Australian aborigines. Intelligence tests can never be culture-free; they inevitably reflect the background of experience and skills considered important by the testers. Again, different peoples will approach tests with different degrees of sophistication and will expend different amounts of mental energy and perseverance upon them. Their motivation may be extremely difficult to assess and may be quite different from that of their examiners.

Intelligence, then, however defined, must involve a complex of characters under the control of several genes. Environment, too, will have a contribution to make, and this will more often be susceptible to measurement.

Whilst the inheritance of differences between individuals which are known to be controlled by one gene, or a very few genes, can usually be predicted, those controlling the complicated response patterns involved in intelligence, being numerous, are less susceptible to precise analysis.

We do know, however, that in certain circumstances a single gene difference may determine severe mental retardation, and the biochemical and physiological pathways by which this occurs can be described.

The disease phenylketonuria (PKU) is caused by an individual receiving from both parents a mutated or changed gene that is normally responsible for controlling the enzyme that routinely alters one of the body's amino-acids, phenylalanine, into another, tyrosine. Unfortunately the mutant gene allows the phenylalanine level to build up in the blood and in the brain, thus causing severe mental retardation. Only to a limited extent can any medical intervention be made, by instituting in early life a special diet deficient in phenylalanine, thus reducing its accumulation.

If we measure the amounts of phenylalanine in the blood of PKU sufferers and in normal people, there is a clear-cut difference, genetically-determined, separating the two groups. If conventional intelligence tests are administered to both there is, despite a very small overlap, again a clear distinction that can be made on a basis of their test scores. The small overlap merely indicates that the very "brightest" PKU sufferers are marginally "brighter" than the "dullest" normal people.

The PKU genotype manifests itself in at least two other ways. If head size (head length plus head breadth) is examined, phenylketonurics are found to have smaller heads, on average, than normal people. Although the difference is a statistically valid one, there is considerable overlap between the ranges for each group of people. Thus normal individuals fall between about 310 and 370 millimetres, whilst phenylketonurics fall between about 260 and 350 millimetres, the respective means being about 330 and 320 millimetres. Thus although the PKU genotype is clearly responsible for the group difference, it is not possible to allot, on this mean basis alone, an individual with a head size of, say, 323 millimetres to one group or the other. This is in contrast to the clear-cut distinction that can be made on the basis of phenylalanine levels in blood plasma samples.

Another PKU manifestation is in hair colour. Hair colour can be measured objectively by means of the spectrophotometer. This instrument directs a beam of light onto the hair surface, and measures the incident light reflected by the hair at some selected wavelength. The percentage of light reflected is always greater towards the red end of the visible spectrum than towards the blue, where wavelengths are shorter. A pale skin reflects light more effectively than a dark one. Phenylketonurics, on average, reflect more light from their hair than do normal subjects, although, as in the case of head size, there is considerable overlap between ranges for the two groups. So, again, although a statistically significant difference occurs in hair colour, an individual cannot be placed confidently within one group or the other on the basis of this one character.

Looking at our four variables, then, we can say that the genetic difference between PKU sufferers and normal people importantly affects their blood phenylalanine levels, and their intelligence, but only marginally affects head size and hair colour, significant though the average differences may be.

Today, a routine urine test of babies screens out the phenylketonurics early in life. The genotype is fortunately quite rare; out of a million people, only 100 will suffer from this genetic disorder. Despite its demonstrated effect upon intelligence, then, it will have virtually no effect upon the average intelligence quotient of the population within which it is found.

We learn further from the PKU situation that here is a gene whose effects may be much modified by environment. We know this from the observation of the variation that exists between individual phenylketonurics. Thus the PKU gene is responsible initially for the aberrant phenylalanine values in the blood, but a deliberate environmental influence such as nutrition deficient in phenylalanine can markedly modify these values. Again, an individual may receive only one PKU gene from his parents. His mental abilities as a result may not be drastically impaired, although a blood examination may reveal higher-than-normal phenylalanine levels. Clearly, then, a genetic component interacting with the nutritional (or environmental) one is responsible for the disorder.

A gene that can vary in its characteristics in this way is referred to as a polymorphic one—one that can have more than one morphology, shape or form. The several genes probably responsible for intelligence are likely to be polymorphisms, working in concert, but individually varying in their effect, much in the same way that the PKU genotype varies phenotypically in head size and hair colour. Thus, whilst individual genetic variation may be difficult to quantify, or even identify, the total result of the interaction of the assembly of genes responsible for intelligence may be unmistakable and measurable. With polymorphic systems of this kind, quantitative division of responsibility between heredity and environment is extremely difficult to accomplish.

But, although very difficult, it is not completely impossible. One extremely useful method is by means of the study of twins. Twins are of two kinds, identical and non-identical. Identical (or monozygotic) twins are derived from the same fertilized egg. They are therefore of the same sex, and have the same genetic identity. If differences arise as they develop, they must therefore be the product of the environment. Non-identical (or dizygotic) twins, on the other hand, are derived from two eggs, each fertilized by a different sperm. Although this fertilization took place at the same time, the two non-identical twins will differ genetically as much as any other brothers or sisters would differ.

Twins brought up within a normal family environment will be subjected to virtually identical environmental stimuli and pressures. If for any reason they are separated at birth and reared apart, then their environmental stimuli are likely to differ.

Several revealing comparisons can be made through the utilization of twin studies, and an attempt can be made to assess the contributions of heredity and environment to certain characters. A common technique of inquiry is by means of a correlation coefficient. A mathematical formula allows the investigator to examine the closeness of fit between data for any two individuals or two groups. A coefficient of zero implies no correlation at all, whilst a coefficient of 1.0 would indicate complete correlation. Suppose we examined identical twins, brought up at home together, for characters such as height and weight. We should expect to find the figures to be very similar for both twins, assuming they had regularly eaten similar diets. The correlation here might be as high as 0.9. A component of each character would be heredity, another would depend upon the amounts of diet and exercise. If, on the other hand, they had been separated at birth, and adopted and brought up in different families, then their height and weight might differ quite markedly, reflecting differences in upbringing, but not in genetic background. The same would be true for intellectual qualities and abilities measured by intelligence tests. The socio-economic status of each household, its attitude to education, its cultural background—these would combine as environmental factors tending to bring about disparity in I.Q. scores. How important is heredity in this matter? What is the extent of its contribution?

It is difficult to be sure. A major unknown quantity is the amount of interaction between genotype and environment. Whilst we know little that is precise about such interaction, it is clear that the possibility exists that certain genotypes develop better in one environment than in another. But conclusions drawn in one population sample regarding this may be quite invalid in another that comes under scrutiny. All that can really be said is that the numerous studies carried out suggest that the heritability of intelligence is fairly high—at least 50 per cent, and even as high as 80 per cent, if heritability is regarded in its broadest sense.

Research carried out in London, England, by Professor Cyril Burt, and published in 1961, has revealed consistent differences in mean I.Q. between the various socio-economic strata of an urban population. Between the mean for the highest social group (comprising professors, lawyers, doctors and so on) and that of the lowest (manual workers, unskilled labourers), there is a gap of some 50 I.Q. units. Intelligence, then, as measured by conventional tests, appears to be closely related to social class and occupation. Furthermore, the same kind of difference appears when children of parents of the different socio-economic strata are tested.

It is clear, then, that differences in intelligence as measured by conventional I.Q. tests between individuals do exist. Differences in intelligence between groups of people have also been shown to exist. Can the argument be taken a stage further—can "racial" differences in intelligence be demonstrated to exist? Obviously differences between individuals, whatever their racial affinities might be, are going to exist. But what about means for intelligence quotients derived from large population samples of different racial affinities?

Let us first look briefly at some of the most commonly quoted evidence—that relating to U.S. Blacks and Whites —before turning to the evidence available concerning comparisons of Canadian Indians and Canadian Whites.

It is well known that many investigations in the U.S. have reported differences in the mean I.Q. of U.S. Blacks and U.S. Whites. Means for U.S. Whites generally run between 10 and 20 I.Q. units higher than for U.S. Blacks. A study by Kennedy and others of Florida State University in 1963, involving the I.Q. testing of some 1,800 Black elementary school-children from five southern states (Florida, Georgia, Alabama, Tennessee, and S. Carolina), revealed a mean I.Q. of 80.7, with a standard deviation of 12.4. A 1960 study of a U.S. White sample gave a mean I.Q. of 101.3, with a standard deviation of 16.4. This indicates a difference between means of 21.1, one of the highest such differences as yet reported.

However, if one distribution curve is superimposed upon the other, then a considerable overlap is evident. In fact, the lowest Black scores are not much lower than the lowest Whites scores and the highest Black scores are virtually identical to the highest Whites scores.

The U.S. Army "alpha" intelligence tests, widely administered in connection with enlistment in the armed forces, have shown that Blacks from northern U.S. states often score higher than Whites from southern states. Clearly environment, particular home background and quality and quantity of educational opportunities, exert influence on these results.

The possibility that racial discrimination itself can affect I.Q. scores has also been investigated. Psychologists have recently become much impressed by the hypothesis that the individual characteristics of the person administering the test can actually affect how well a subject will perform in it. Even as early as 1936 it was known that when the I.Q. of U.S. Blacks was tested by White and Black testers, the Blacks scored, on average, six I.Q. units lower when tested by White examiners. Several other studies after that date have confirmed these early findings. The race of the tester made a real difference in results; Blacks being tested by Whites found it a more stressful situation than that of being tested by Blacks. Such stress appeared to affect their motivation and their "possibility of success".

Intelligence tests have been conducted on a world-wide basis for many years in an effort to elucidate this problem of race and intelligence. The results seem to point to certain very general conclusions. The culture of the population being studied appears greatly to affect average scores. Tests found useful in one culture are often completely inappropriate in another. Social custom may affect motivation in tests, so that in one culture individuals may strive for personal success, whilst in others they may have been taught to avoid it. Survival may have been facilitated in some communities by a pretence of stupidity in the presence of superiors. Nutritional status and health status will affect test results. It is difficult, if not impossible, then, to weigh the many imponderable variables, and attempts objectively to relate human genetics and intelligence in situations of this kind are clearly premature. They may well remain so.

Let us next, in the light of these tentative findings, look at the case of the Indians in Canada, with specific regard to work done on their intelligence compared with that of their white peer-groups. We shall see that there are some interesting parallels with experience in other lands and with other peoples.

The Asiatic origin of the Indians and their prehistory and history in Canada is considered in more detail in the next chapter. Basically, five distinctive ecological areas can be distinguished in Canada, reflecting a background of differing Indian cultural traditions. It is important to

bear in mind that there has never been a homogeneous
Indian tradition as such; Indians became widely dispersed,
and thus heterogeneous, subsequent to their arrival in the
New World. Their entry is a story of many migrations.
There are also many sociological and socio-economic
differences between Canada's Indians. Some remain hunters to this day, whilst others have successfully joined the
ranks of Canada's professionals.

The 1971 Census of Canada lists, under the heading
"Population by Mother Tongue—Indian and Eskimo",
179,825 persons. Subtracting the 13,000 Eskimos gives us
an approximate total of some 166,000 "status" Indians
(to this total must be added "non-status" Indians and
Indians for whom English or French is the mother tongue).
This Canadian Indian population is divided into some 500
"bands", having access to over 2,000 Indian reserves.

It is now generally recognized throughout Canada that
the Indians have long been neglected, and that as a result,
their socio-economic status, when considered as a whole,
is far below that of other Canadian citizens (with the exception of the Eskimos). Energetic government efforts
have and are being made to improve the Indians' status,
mainly through concern with social welfare, economic
development and, most importantly, through education.
It is only through improvements in education that the
Indian can hope to compete with non-Indians for employment off the reserves.

The Hawthorne Report (1967) is an invaluable source
of information regarding the impact of education upon the
Canadian Indian and his attitudes in response to it. Much
of the remainder of this chapter is drawn from its findings.
Amongst other matters, the Report attempts to account
for "the lack of achievement, low levels of aspiration and
negative self-image of Indian youth".

From the data collected by the Report's investigators,
it was clear to them that schooling for the typical Indian
child represents a basic discontinuity in his life-experience.
So traumatic was this impact, that it was considered to
account for the retardation of 80 per cent of Indian chil-

dren in their first school grade, and to account for an average age-grade retardation of at least two and a half years for all Indian school children.

Life-experience for children, prior to their coming to school for the first time, is basically experience derived from home and family, and from their community. That school-life represents a discontinuity in this experience is attributable to the difference in educational background of Indian parents compared to that of non-Indian parents. There are typically different expectations from life, different socialization processes and different values." Economic backgrounds usually differed greatly, with Indian children more often living in overcrowded home conditions, and suffering from bad health and inadequate food. Where Indian culture was flourishing and the Indian way of life still accepted and respected, there conventional schooling was less highly regarded. Formal education was seen as being irrelevant, when Indians were still able to secure economic success and achieve status through traditional Indian occupations. Attitudes of non-Indian neighbours towards Indians affected the self-image and aspirations of the latter. It was noticed, too, that without semi-professional or professional examples to look up to, Indians tended to regard themselves as destined to work at logging, fishing and various semi-skilled or unskilled occupations, often only seasonal, with which they had become familiar in their daily lives.

It would thus be misleading to assume that because certain similarities are observed between the classroom behaviour and attitudes of Indian school children and non-Indian low socio-economic group school children, that the basic problem is simply one of poverty. Urban slum areas may well be far bleaker and deprived environments than that of the Indian home under discussion. Many Indian children have been exposed to a rich tradition of language and culture within their own group. It is unfortunate, however, that this can do little to prepare them for sudden immersion in conventional school life with its inimical values and activities.

There are many and different reactions by Indian children to this exposure to school discipline and timetables. Absenteeism of Indian children is a major problem, and reflects both unhappiness with the school situation, and the frequent economic demand for child labour on the reserves. The reported range for Indian absenteeism is between 10 and 100 days of a 180-day school year, with an average absence of 40 days. The amount of individual absenteeism increases with each year spent in school.

School-related problems resulting in absenteeism are many. They range from fear of the teacher, ridicule by non-Indian peers, academic failure, inadequate or inappropriate clothing, to hunger and lack of pocket money.

Home-related problems may include kin obligations such as baby-sitting, household chores, assistance required in hunting, fishing and in seasonal employment such as crop-picking. Indian patterns of living may be mobile; they may involve domestic timetables at variance with those expected by the school.

Earlier in this chapter it was pointed out that there is psychological evidence that the attitudes of non-Blacks to Blacks had an effect upon the latter, and lowered their test scores in intelligence tests when Whites were the examiners. It is clear, too, that in Canada the attitudes of non-Indians towards Indians powerfully affect the latter, and modify their attitude towards themselves. Modified also in this way is their appreciation of possibilities for success away from the reserves, and their appreciation of what they are "worth", when measured against the major Canadian community.

Let us look finally, then, in this chapter, in connection with race and intelligence, at what we know of the results of intelligence tests carried out on Canadian Indians, and how these results can be interpreted.

Many Canadian teachers believe that the backwardness of Indian students is amply demonstrated not only by their poor academic progress in general but by their consistently low I.Q. test scores. Some teachers, more enlightened than others, are aware of the difficulties involved in this kind of testing, and are aware that the tests might simply be inappropriate when used on Indian children. Whilst it is repugnant to suggest innate or genetic differences between Indian and non-Indian in characters affecting intelligence as conventionally measured, teachers generally do not expect Indian students to do well in school or to perform well in I.Q. tests.

The following quotation taken from the Hawthorne Report underlines the incongruity of using I.Q. tests developed from standards applicable to English-speaking White middle-class urban students to assess the potential abilities of Canadian Indian students:

One example of the misuses of the tests may suffice to make the point that the tests are not useful with minority group children and that a great deal of harm is done by using and recording them. In community X 1,400 students were given two tests: the Otis Quick Scoring and the California Test of Mental Maturity. Both are paper and pencil tests and both purport to measure achievement and intelligence. The tests were administered by the staff of a regional mental health clinic who had never been to community X before; their testing trip took three days which they spent in the school. Of the 1,400 students, 189 were Indians from the local reserve. When the tests were completed, 200 children were classified as 'ineducable' which means that they should have special education not normally provided in the average school. Of the 200 considered 'ineducable', 164 were Indian. Of a total Indian student enrolment of 189, 164 were considered 'ineducable'.

The tests are given to all children at the beginning of grade one and at the end of grade one as well as in other grades throughout the school life of the child. Results are entered on the student's Permanent Record Card and follow him from class to class and from school to school. Even if a teacher is aware that test results may not be accurate, it would be difficult for him to look at a series of below normal scores on a child's PRC and not conclude that the child has low ability. If school systems had adequate facilities for slow learners, almost every Indian child in the country would be in one on the basis of his intelligence and achievement test results (p. 144).

The Report further points out that the Indian children came from a hunting-trapping reserve, with a history of much seasonal employment. The majority of these reserve Indians spoke only Cree, and most of the first-grade school-children also only spoke Cree. "With the exception of the superintendent for Indian schools for the area, no one questioned the test results. They were duly recorded on the children's PRC's."

With a record of failure in the first grade, and with no real opportunity to succeed under the present educational system, there seems little chance for many Canadian Indian children to break free from this bondage. From the foregoing it will be realized that the primary reasons for failure are social and cultural rather than intellectual. To rectify this state of affairs is a dynamic challenge to Canada's teachers and Indian Affairs administrators. Fortunately there are signs that respect for educational achievement, and for success in making a way of life off the reserve, are increasing in many Indian communities. As more and more important negotiations with government agencies occur (in connection with land rights, for example), so social awareness grows, and the way of life of the wider world around the reserves makes a more prominent impression, especially amongst the young.

One Canadian experiment, in response to the kind of difficulty experienced by many Canadian Indian school-children, that is particularly relevant here is that carried out in Nova Scotia with a pre-school programme for "culturally deprived" Black children in Halifax. The experiment has been at least partially successful in giving Black children from a lower-class disadvantaged background social and cultural stimulation considered to be lacking in their homes, and considered to be one of the advantages enjoyed by children entering school from a White middle-class background (Clark, 1967).

This, and similar experiments such as the "Head Start" programme in the U.S.A., immediately bring up a current strident controversy in psychological circles, involving particularly Professor A. R. Jensen of the University of California at Berkeley. He vigorously asserts that compensatory education of this kind can be shown to have failed. For the background of this argument, and other contemporary ones surrounding race and intelligence, heredity and race, the reader is directed elsewhere (Richardson & Spears, 1972).

We return, then, in the controversy surrounding race and intelligence, to the question of whether nature or nurture, genotype or environment, is more important in determining the development or potential development of any people. It appears clear, at least in these terms, that innate endowment is perhaps insufficient; environment must provide the opportunity for such endowment to emerge and develop, and the opportunity must be there if the fullest potential is to be realized. What, one may wonder, would have happened to Shakespeare if he had never learned to write? Let us take another example: consider what happens when the farmer sows seed. Some may fall on stony ground, and some on fertile earth. Genetically speaking, the seeds are identical, having come from one source. The sickly poor development, on the one hand, and the vigorous growth on the other, demonstrates again the importance of environment, and how it may well be more influential than heredity.

However, the problem, although one of great general concern, must be admitted today to be one that is not clearly susceptible to proof, at least through the present systems of inquiry that exist within the area of human biology.

Chapter 5

The Peoples of Canada Today

To understand how Canada became populated by man we must first understand the peopling of the Americas as a whole. To do this, we must look at the evidence that is available indicating when man came to the New World, what kind of man he was, and how he spread after he arrived here. Such evidence is largely archaeological, consisting of cultural remains such as artefacts, hunting camps, occupation sites and hearths. In addition, but all too rarely, skeletal remains of some of these earliest Americans have been recovered.

Until fairly recently, estimates concerning the date of the arrival of man in South America suggested that it happened some 14,000 years ago. New archaeological findings in the highlands of Peru, however, have now suggested that man's arrival there can be pushed back to at least 22,000 years ago. The nature of the stone tools associated with these newly-found Andean hunting cultures suggests that they were derived from earlier types of tools, thus indicating to some scholars that the appearance of man in the Americas might well lie between 40,000 and 100,000 years ago. This is much farther in the past than has previously been suggested by archaeologists.

No human skeletal remains have been recovered from these early Andean sites. However, a comparison of the artefacts with material from the Old World supports the view that these immigrants came to the Americas from Asia, entering by what is now Alaska.

Turning for a moment to the evidence of geology, it will be realized from the foregoing remarks that man did not appear in the New World until Upper Pleistocene times. At various times during the Pleistocene a broad expanse of land (the Bering "land-bridge") connected Siberia with North America. These periodic land bridges were created by drops in sea level associated with the fluctuations of prevailing glaciations. As a glaciation extended its ice-cover, so sea levels would drop; as the glaciated area shrank and water accumulated, so sea levels would rise again, submerging previously exposed coastlines. It appears that steppe-adapted animals such as the horse were able to cross between Siberia and North America in these glacial times, but man was the first modern primate to attempt the move. He was only able to do so when his technology had developed to a point at which he could support himself, on a long-term basis, in a cold environment.

Having entered North America, however, man was to move forward rapidly, taking advantage of the large herds of animals that were to be found. Now-extinct species of horses, llamas, ground sloths, camels, mastodons and mammoths flourished in great numbers at this time. Archaeological evidence accordingly shows widespread hunting activity by man in the Americas between 13,000 and 15,000 years ago. Such Paleo-Indian cultures lasted in some localities until about 10,000 years ago, and are associated with distinctive Clovis and Folsom projectile points, called after sites where they were first found.

There is much evidence of "pre-projectile" cultures, from places as far apart as California, Texas, Mexico and Peru, and also from Old Crow in the Canadian Yukon. These people from Old Crow, living there about 25,000 years ago, can probably be called the first "Canadians."

As the Pleistocene climate slowly changed, and the mammoths and other cold-adapted animals retreated with the ice sheets, so big game generally became scarcer; indeed, the predatory activities of man the hunter certainly accelerated the process of extinction of many of these animals. It has been estimated that within 6,000 years thirty-five mammalian genera were exterminated in North America. As man increased in number, so more and more animals were killed off, eventually leaving only deer, caribou and bison to survive.

Replacing the big-game hunting culture, identified by the distinctive projectile points, came the so-called Woodland culture, characterized by pottery resembling that of northern Asia, and having ground stone axes, bifacially chipped knives, and projectile points. It is a very homogeneous culture, suggesting recent development, and is widespread in North America, extending into Canada. Linguistic evidence supports this cultural homogeneity, for if we look at languages spoken by living Indians of north and north-eastern North America, we find only two major divisions, Algonkian and Athabascan, with Iroquoian as a minor linguistic intrusion.

In parallel with this third cultural phase, must be placed the distinctive Arctic Eskimo culture that was now developing along the circumpolar land margins from Siberia, through Alaska and Arctic Canada, to Greenland. This culture, essentially based on a marine-hunting economy, probably evolved from a neolithic Asian Pacific coast culture. There are resemblances, for example, to early Hokkaido culture in the north of Japan. Thus these Eskimos were the next "Canadians" to arrive at and enter what are our present boundaries.

What did these early peoples of the Americas look like? This fascinating problem can only be approached by a study of the available skeletal evidence, and this is not extensive until the arrival on the scene of the better-represented peoples associated with the Woodland culture.

The earliest skeletal remains of man in the Americas (with their probable antiquity) include those from Tepexpan, Mexico, (10,000 years old), Marmes, Oregon (11,000 years old), Midland, Texas (between 14,000 and 20,000 years old), Laguna Beach, California (17,000 years old), and "Los Angeles Man" (23,000 years old). When these remains are studied, the general impression is that they differ very little from skeletal remains of recent Amerindian peoples. They are all clearly *Homo sapiens*.

In Canada, the remains of an infant have been found at Tabor Hill, Alberta, tentatively suggested as being between 30,000 and 60,000 years old. Assuming this dating to be reliable, then these remains would represent the earliest known skeletal evidence of man in the Americas. Little can be said of the biological affinities of incomplete and immature remains of this kind, but they undoubtedly are of *Homo sapiens*.

It would in fact be surprising, in view of the suggested dates for man's first arrival in the Americas, that he would be of any earlier human species such as *Homo erectus*. By the time man arrived in America, he had fully evolved elsewhere in the world into man like ourselves. We should not overlook the fact, however, that the Amerindian population today is very diverse in physical type and it might be expected to differ, as it does in certain aspects of morphology, from its Asian ancestors. Taking into account the Asian origin of the American indigenous peoples, we can make a simple dichotomy on a basis of biological criteria between "paleo-Mongoloid" peoples such as the American Indians and "neo-Mongoloid" peoples such as the Eskimos and the Aleut, reflecting the considerable time interval separating their respective arrivals in the New World. It is entirely to be expected, therefore, that although both groups of people basically belong to the Mongoloid major division of mankind, the physical and genetical resemblances between many Amerindian groups and Mongoloid peoples in Asia today, will be less than those between Eskimos and such Asians.

When we think of Canada and its people, particularly the recent arrivals in our land, we tend conveniently to forget that *all* Canadians are immigrants, or are descended from immigrants. And, against the backdrop of man's first arrival in the Americas, peoples from Europe have been here only a very short time. Peoples from Asia preceded them by some tens of thousands of years. To be sure, the creation of what we now call Canada was largely accomplished by people of European ancestry, but our population today comprises peoples who were here before them, as well as many peoples who came after them.

As has already been pointed out, the arrival of man in the Americas is a comparatively recent episode in the evolution, differentiation and dispersion of *Homo sapiens*. Man in the Americas, then, played no part in the dramatic evolution of "men-like-apes" into "men-like-ourselves". He came here fully formed, in every way a true representative of *Homo sapiens*. This situation has, of course, remained unchanged throughout the subsequent waves of immigration, primarily from Europe and eventually from Africa, and many other parts of the world. Ironically, perhaps, some of the most recent immigrants to Canada, as well as to other parts of the Americas, have been again from the Asian homeland referred to at the start of this chapter, thus stressing the recent restless mobility of our human species as environmental stresses such as population pressure grow.

The somewhat wary attitudes of many of Canada's peoples towards each other, in terms usually of their real or fictitious origins and the stereotypes associated with these, are dealt with more fully in the next chapters of this book. Let us see, however, how the physical anthropologist and human biologist, engaged in the unravelling of man's biological affinities and relationships, regards the scientific validity of some of these attitudes that people have expressed towards one another.

The first thing he would do is to stress the biological unity of man today within one human species. What do we mean here by "unity"? Our human species is a closed genetic system; that is to say our species is unable to hybridize with any other. This is because there exists now no other species of the genus *Homo*; in fact, none has

existed for probably a quarter of a million years. For reproductive purposes, therefore, our species is restricted to its
own living members. That there is no biological barrier to
reproduction between any of the world's peoples is abund-
antly clear from our history, and from the many examples
alive today. (An exception should be made, of course, in
unavoidable cases of sterility or infertility.) This has led,
as we pointed out in an earlier chapter, to the appearance,
through the development of the world's peoples, of "new"
populations such as the Canadian Métis and American
Blacks, the latter being also represented in Canada.

This process of hybridization or miscegenation implies
a biological overlap of gene pools, introducing through
reproduction, genes, perhaps numerous in one population,
into another, where they may be rare or even absent. The
overall effect then is to broaden the spectrum of human
variability. It is important to recognize this process not as
one of blending characteristics, but as bringing forward
new combinations or permutations of genes. Thus a new
gene pool, such as that possessed by Canada's Métis, will
include genes characteristic of Canadian Indian peoples as
well as those derived from Canada's British and French
settlers. The test of whether such miscegenation is viable
or not is a simple one—reproductive success. The answer
is clear.

We must not lose sight of the fact that despite there
being no convincing biological argument within our species
against miscegenation, the reasons for it occurring (or not
occurring) are more likely to be socio-cultural ones. Thus,
marriage often provides upward social mobility for a
partner of lower status. Socio-cultural "barriers" to miscegenation will include what might be referred to as "high
visibility" ones such as disparate skin pigmentation, and
those of less obvious immediate visibility such as religion
or language.

Looking at what is commonly called our Canadian
ethnic "mosaic", there is a tendency all too often to think
in terms of stereotypes, and to think of particular ethnic
groups as virtually discrete and homogenous "racial"

units. Certainly some groups are notably more endogamous than others—Canada's indigenous peoples, for example—whilst the French, Italians and Jews, being prominently conscious of their "ethnicity", also have reportedly high percentages of marriages taking place within their own group. Only about half the marriages among Germans, Polish and Dutch in Canada, on the other hand, are endogamous according to Census data. Ethnic stereotypes are often reinforced by significant differences in the degree of representation within certain industries and occupations. Thus, compared to the national employment average, the Germans, Ukrainians and Dutch have proportionately more adult males working in agriculture, the French in forestry, the Italians in building construction, the Polish in manufacturing, and Indian and Métis in fishing and trapping.

One of the contemporary tasks of the physical anthropologist is to attempt to demonstrate the biological affinities between the populations of man. Depending upon the nature and amount of evidence available, such assessments may range in complexity from a simple comparison of bony or toothy remains to elaborate statistical treatment of gene frequencies and measurements, designed to produce estimates of "genetic distance" between human groups. Techniques such as factor analysis can be used with profit, and three-dimensional models can be constructed to demonstrate inter-populational human relationships in a multi-dimensional space.

What do we know of the origin of Canada's many immigrant groups? In terms of numerical strength, the two "charter" groups, British and French, are predominant. About 43 per cent of Canadians are of British ethnic origins, and about 31 per cent are of French origins. The term "British" comprises, of course, people who would describe themselves as English, Scots, Irish or Welsh (not to mention Cornish or Manx). United in their homeland, in a political sense (except for Eire), and by the use of a common lingua franca, they nevertheless can be shown to possess significant phenotypic and genotypic heterogeneity. Consider what Daniel Defoe, writing in 1701, had to say about the origins of the English: "Who are the English . . . ." he asked:

> . . . who despise the Dutch,
> And rail at new-come foreigners so much;
> Forgetting that themselves are all derived
> From the most scoundrel race that ever lived,
> A horrid crowd of rambling thieves and drones,
> Who ransacked kingdoms and dispeopled towns:
> The Pict and painted Briton, treacherous Scot,
> By hunger, theft and rapine either brought;
> Norwegian pirates, buccaneering Danes,
> Whose red-haired offspring everywhere remains;
> Who, joined with Norman-French compound the breed
> from whence your true-born Englishmen proceed.

The racial history of Britain is far too complex to go into here in any detail (see Hughes & Brothwell, 1968). All that we know of it, however, echoes the sentiments expressed by Defoe. One is led, inevitably, to the conclusion that terms such as "Anglo-Saxon" are, by today, virtually meaningless, although perennially used in such Canadian contractions as "W.A.S.P." (White/Anglo-Saxon/Protestant). Britain's history is one of much immigration and ceaseless mobility. Some broad distinctions can be made; for example, between Celtic peoples coming from Central Europe and the Mediterranean, and later arrivals of non-Celtic immigrants from Scandinavia and other parts of Northern Europe. In terms of racial history, clearly, the "English" are comparative newcomers to British shores.

In connexion with the emphasis placed in the literature surrounding the British North America Act upon the "two founding races", it is of interest to examine what we know of some of the skeins of racial history that inextricably entwine these two peoples.

It is approximately between 40,000 B.C. and 26,000 B.C. that we find skeletal remains in Europe that more or less resemble contemporary peoples of the area. Earlier populations of neandertaloid types of man were replaced during this period by men, coming probably from the Middle East, and spreading out over most of Western and Eastern Europe, Western Asia and Northern Africa. These people of the Upper Pleistocene Age were to evolve in the course of time into Mesolithic (Middle Stone Age) and Neolithic (New Stone Age) villagers, and into the various better-known tribes of the Bronze and Iron Ages.*

The ecological changes initiated during the Mesolithic period continued into the Neolithic period, which is prominently characterized by the adoption of agriculture and animal husbandry. As the glaciers of Europe continued to shrink towards Scandinavia, so the once well-watered grasslands moved in response, so that areas such as what is now Iran became dessicated, and the fertile Nile valley became swampy and inimical to man.

A result of these ecological changes was a mass migration of peoples, a movement that had begun in Mesolithic times and which now received a fresh impetus from newly-learned agricultural techniques. Palestine, North Africa and southern Europe were the first to experience this immigration, Neolithic farmers eventually spreading over most of Western Europe and reaching Britain. Such migration came from the south and east, and these immigrant populations were to form the basis from which the present populations of Europe are descended.

In Britain, the remains of Megalithic or Long Barrow peoples (so named from the shape of their burial grounds) represent the periphery of the Neolithic population expansion, and there is close morphological similarity beween these British Long Barrow people and certain of the French Neolithic people, for example those represented by skeletal remains in the corridor tombs of Vadancourt, Oise.

As the Neolithic was replaced by the Bronze and Iron Ages, so many population shifts occurred in Western Europe. The Bell Beaker people (so named after a distinctive pottery type) arrived in Britain from Northern

* See Table 2, Chapter 1, p. 12, for further clarification.

Europe, and, choosing to settle in areas occupied by Long Barrow people, probably hybridized with them.

By the close of the Bronze Age the racial situation in Western Europe was to be that of an initial stratum of long-headed peoples, mainly of Mediterranean origins, being infiltrated by round-headed peoples coming from Eastern Europe. Much of the racial history of these times is obscured, however, by the Late Bronze Age custom of cremating their dead rather than burying them. Cremated human remains are difficult to study.

Normal interment was resumed during the Iron Age in Europe—about 700 B.C. Sizeable Celtic population apparently lived in France and in Britain at that date. The cranial evidence shows these Celts to be moderately round-headed, with sloping foreheads, long faces and prominent noses. But it should be emphasized that almost any Celtic population selected for examination will show a proportion of aberrant individuals, representing survivals of older populations, accretions of emerging populations other than Celtic ones, and hybridization.

The subsequent invasions of Britain by peoples such as the Angles, Saxons, Jutes, and the incursions of Caesar's legions, were to push many of these Celtic peoples towards the periphery of the British islands—into Wales, Scotland and Ireland. The Norman Conquest was to bring a French royal court to England. Celtic peoples from Cornwall were to emigrate to Brittany in France from where, as Breton fishermen and sailors, as chance would have it, they were to arrive eventually in Canada as the first representatives of France to settle in this country.

The two "founding races", therefore, although identifiable by linguistic and other cultural criteria, can be seen to possess many elements of a common racial heritage.

All the foregoing is not to deny, of course, that the gene pools of the French-Canadian and British-Canadian populations today will be found to differ. The French-Canadian community has maintained itself, in a biological sense, by endogamy and large families. This process, over time, is certain to have encouraged a degree of genetic homogeneity, and has produced distinctive frequencies of many genes (say for the blood-group systems), and even a distinctive morphology. The British-Canadian community, on the other hand, has maintained itself more by continued immigration from the homeland, so that its gene pool reflects the composition of that of contemporary Britain. Much of what has been said in connexion with aspects of Europe's racial history is relevant, too, in explaining the origins of many other Canadian peoples, such as the Germans, Ukrainians, Italians and the Dutch. The rise of nationalism in Europe, the preoccupation with political, linguistic, religious, and cultural boundaries have all tended to obscure the genetic heritage common to all these peoples. Some broad distinctions can, of course, be made when we look at the peoples of Europe today. On a basis of, say, skin and hair pigmentation, it is relatively easy to distinguish northern Europeans such as Swedes or Norwegians from southern Europeans such as Spaniards or Italians. It is important, however, to recognize the clinal (or continuous) nature of such pigmentary variation. There are rarely any discrete boundaries between adjacent populations, whether morphological or genetic characters are considered. Thus, as we travel southwards in Europe from Scandinavia, for example, skin and hair colour slowly become darker as southerly latitudes are passed. We find as we look at a Canadian ethnic group that a spectrum of human variability is being displayed. Names are often merely classificatory conveniences. Thus, when we speak of "Germans" in Canada, we overlook that such a category will include people originally coming from Russia, Russian Poland, Hungary, Roumania and many parts of what was once the Austro-Hungarian Empire. When we speak of "Icelanders" in Canada, we imply that their origin was in Iceland, and when we look more closely at that, we learn that the island was settled by Norse immigrants from Scandinavia and by Irish from Britain. We tend to assume that "Italians" in Canada are a homogeneous population, overlooking often the morphological and genetical differences between the peoples of the north of Italy and those of the south, and of Sicily.

One distinctively Canadian population about whose evolution we can be far more certain is that of the Métis. The term *métis*, meaning "mixed" is a French cognate of the Spanish term *mestizo*. The mixture referred to is that resulting from intermarriage between people of European origin (mainly French Canadian) and indigenous Canadian peoples such as the Cree Indians. In some cases, notably in the Mackenzie Delta and adjacent coasts, near Sachs Harbour and Banks Island, the hybridization may be European-Eskimo or Eskimo-Indian-European. It is only to be expected that as the process of the development of Canada's North continues, and as acculturation of Indians and Eskimos proceeds, so this kind of miscegenation will also increase in years to come. Slobodin (1971), writing of the Métis, differentiates between the Red River Métis and the Northern Métis, explaining their different hybrid origins. The Red River Métis are the result of relatively remote miscegenation, their European genes being derived from French Canadians or gallicized Scots and Irish, and their indigenous genes being derived from Algonkians, such as Cree, Ojibway or Saulteaux, from Iroquoians (Six Nations) or Athabaskan of the Slave region such as Chipewyan and Slave Dogrib. They are a coherent community, with a long history, and recognize few Indian or European kin.

The Northern Métis are derived from relatively recent miscegenation between mainly Scots, Scandinavians and English, and Athabaskan Indians such as the Bear Lake, Hare, Kutchin and Dogrib peoples, as well as western Arctic Eskimos. They recognize appreciable numbers of White, Indian and Eskimo kin. As might be expected from these differences there are major social, religious and other cultural distinctions between the two groups. The Jewish people form another interesting example of miscegenation over the centuries following their dispersion (the Diaspora) beginning in A.D. 70. The American anthropologist, H. L. Shapiro, has commented succinctly upon their biological history in these words.

"Through their dispersion they remained a world people, enormously expanding their geographical and social contacts. Few other peoples in modern times have had consequently so varied a biological history. As a result they have contributed something of their genetic heritage to perhaps more different people than any other group and have, in return, absorbed an equal number of new genetic strains, enriching and diversifying themselves" (Shapiro, 1960).

Since the arrival of the first Jews in Canada (in the early years of the 18th century) the same biological process has obviously been going on here, although a large, identifiable fraction has continued to maintain a high degree of social cohesion, through religion, community organization and culture.

Some Canadians are clearly more visible than others, for example the Hutterites of the Prairie Provinces, with their distinctive dress; or the Orthodox Jews of Canada's metropolitan centres. But these imply cultural differences, so that genetically-determined ones, particularly skin and hair pigmentation and hair type stand out even more obviously.

Despite this, Canada's Blacks have generally maintained a low profile since their arrival here. There are estimated to be about 125,000 in Canada with about 35,000 residing in Toronto. Other major communities are found in Montreal, Halifax and Windsor. Most Blacks in fact are urban dwellers, and the majority can trace their ancestry back to the United States. Thus, in Nova Scotia, there are Blacks whose ancestors were Loyalist Negroes who entered the country during the American Revolution; others are descended from refugees of the war of 1812, arriving in British ships from the Chesapeake Bay area; still others are descended from fugitive slaves entering Canada via the "underground railroad" between 1830 and the 1850's. The Jamaican Maroons were taken to Nova Scotia in 1796, and Vancouver Island received Black settlers in 1859. Most recent West Indian migrants went to Toronto, Ottawa and Montreal, with a majority of West Indian students going to the last city. Still other Montreal

Blacks moved into the city in the 1920's from Harlem and other northern urban centres in the U.S.A. Numerically weak, Canada's Blacks have never unified as one group, and West Indians still tend to hold themselves aloof from Blacks of different ancestry. Nevertheless, some prospects for community development at the local level appear to be emerging under new, West Indian leadership as is mentioned later in this book.

In terms of genetic makeup, Canada's Blacks resemble America's Blacks in being by now a virtually "new" race. Estimates made on a basis of genetic markers such as blood-group frequencies have shown that some communities of Blacks in the U.S. possess, by today, up to 30 per cent of genes derived from European and other miscegenation. Frequencies for Canada's Blacks have never been computed, but could not be expected to differ very much. Genetically, therefore, these people now differ from their original ancestors in West Africa, and the process of producing a "new" race, by recombination of genes, will go on as an aspect of man's contemporary evolution.

Canadians of Asian origin are another very "visible" component of our population. They may be divided conveniently into those of Mongoloid ancestry, Chinese and Japanese (and some other minor groups such as Korean), and those of basically Caucasoid ancestry from India and Pakistan. Again, it is their skin colour, and typical morphological phenotype that makes them immediately "visible".

According to the 1971 Census, 118,815 Chinese and 37,260 Japanese live in Canada today, the former people first entering the country during the Frazer River gold rush of the 1850's, and the latter first entering Canada through British Columbia in 1877. It is sad to record that no other racial group has been more persecuted and harassed in the past in Canada than these Mongoloid peoples. They were long considered to be biologically distinct and biologically inferior to most of Canada's other peoples. Today the immense achievements of China and Japan as world powers underline the ludicrousness of this view, as well, of course, as the considerable achievements of Chinese and Japanese within Canada. The two peoples are clearly related as members of the Mongoloid division of mankind and as such are also related to Canada's Eskimos, and, though far more distantly, to the American Indians. Chinese and Japanese, however, have been separated by thousands of years of history, and naturally genetic differences have developed between their representatives today. China, in particular, is an enormous country with a very large population, and thus might be expected to be more heterogeneous in a racial sense than Japan. A common distinction made is that between the taller northern Chinese and the shorter, stockier southern Chinese.

Much more might be said about many of Canada's other ethnic minorities, if space permitted. However, such discussion would revert again and again to the central theme of this portion of the book—that all men differ, one from another, and that population groups also differ, one from another. Variation *within* a group, though, is almost invariably found to be greater than variation *between* human groups.

What then is race? Race, as here defined, refers to and implies any arbitrary classification of human populations, utilizing such biological criteria as actual or assumed physiological and genetic differences between the world's peoples. Other definitions, of course, can also be suggested. It is important to emphasize the words *arbitrary* and *assumed* in the above definition. Too often, as has been shown previously, erroneous labelling of peoples as distinct 'closed' biological groups has been accompanied by equally erroneous value judgements concerning their supposed superiority or inferiority as human beings.

We are, emphatically, members of the only existing human species, but the nature of man is such that he will seldom pause to think logically and objectively about his own kind. His upbringing, his culture and his prejudices come to the foreground, reflecting his basic mistrust of people perceived as different from himself.

These social and culturally determined attitudes are the special concern of the next part of this book.

Chapter 6

Race, Racism and Ethnicity

RACE AND RACISM

The foregoing discussion of the concept of race, emphasizing the biological point of view, indicates that the notion of "pure" or "discrete" human races has little or no scientific justification. Also, many of the commonly-held assumptions as to the "natural", "inherent" or "innate" differences between human populations in morality, intelligence, capacity for culture-building, behaviour patterns, and so on, have nowhere been demonstrated to be scientifically valid.

Why then do people continue to uphold such racist myths? Why do people continue to place so much importance upon *assumed* racial differences? Surely, one might argue, in a modern "enlightened" scientific age, in which public consciousness of racially-defined problems is high, the lack of scientific proof, and the increasing independent evidence of this, should serve to refute these myths.

Unfortunately, scientific knowledge about race is a necessary but not a sufficient condition for the eradication of racist myths. Racism, as defined here, is a social phenomenon which refers to peoples' attitudes, beliefs and behaviour, predicated on non-scientific and erroneous assumptions about the nature of human diversity. Racist myths assume that mankind is divided permanently into a fixed hierarchy of "pure" or discrete races. Within this context, people are assumed to differ in their capacity for being "human". In other words, some peoples are considered less "human", less "evolved", less "civilized" than others. Ideologies of racism, based on such racist myths, rank these mythical races of mankind in an order of superiority and inferiority, usually by standards and criteria that are derived from, and suit, the interests of a particular "race"—viz. the people doing the ranking. It is not surprising, therefore, that in ideologies of racism developed by any one human population, the group doing the ranking will accord to itself the dominant or superordinate position.

For example, ideologies of "White supremacy" developed by European "Whites" depict the "White races"—variously defined—as superior to all other so-called races. At the bottom of this purported scale are the "inferior" Blacks. Their supposed "inferior" or "uncivilized" culture and technology is attributed to an assumed "evolutionary lag" by virtue of which they are deemed incapable of achieving the fullest human development. Such ideologies have served to endow the words "primitive" and "native" with a connotation of innate inferiority, and have served at the same time to legitimate paternalistic attitudes and policies towards people so-defined.

Similarly, the racist ranking order spelled out in the ideology of "anti-Semitism"—an anti-Jewish political movement that arose in Germany in 1873—classified the Germans as supreme. Germans, as then defined, were classified as the elite of the supreme Aryan or Nordic category; all other races were accordingly superseded. Specifically, in this ideology, the Jews were singled out as an "inferior", "vile" and "depraved" "Semitic race"; their very presence in Germany was considered to present a threat of contamination and degeneration to the high level of assumed German civilization. A supposedly scientific foundation for this ideology was provided by the writings of Houston

Stewart Chamberlain (1899) who argued that the Jews were waging a permanent war for the destruction of Aryan civilization, and proclaimed the necessity for "expelling this alien and noxious element from the body of European society". The ideology of anti-Semitism was used to justify repeated acts of hostility towards, and persecution of, Jews in the nineteenth century, and later, to justify the racist policy of genocide that led to the death of six million Jews during World War II, under Hitler's rule in Nazi Germany.

For our present purposes, namely the understanding of the anatomy of racism today, the previous paragraph is instructive. Racist attitudes and beliefs will persist irrespective of their truth or falsity, largely because of their potential usefulness to those in power. Racist ideologies can provide persuasive arguments whereby those in power may attempt to justify and perpetuate existing social, economic and political inequalities between diverse populations, and thereby maintain their position of power.

It seems clear that racism—in ideology and in practice— may bear little or no relationship to the scientific concept of race. It is, therefore, of the utmost importance to distinguish between the scientific and biological concept of race, used for purposes (amongst others) of analyzing populational affinities by measurements of "biological distance", and the unscientific concepts of "pure" race and racism used to perpetuate misconceptions about so-called human differences.

ETHNICITY

In order to distinguish between the definition of race utilizing biological criteria and parallel social definitions, the concept of ethnicity will be used with reference to the arbitrary classification of human populations utilizing both biological and socio-cultural criteria. The concept of ethnicity, like the concept of race, has historically been subject to widespread misinterpretation and misuse. Moreover, adding to the confusion surrounding both concepts is the fact that they have frequently been used interchangeably. Disagreement among scholars as to the "correct" use of these concepts has led some scientists to abandon them.

We argue here that the introduction of new concepts will not necessarily serve to resolve the confusion, but may, in fact, lead to further mystification of our readers. Alternatively, we believe that a precise definition and use of each concept, making explicit the differences between them in criteria utilized for classification, will provide a more fruitful approach to an understanding of the anatomy of racism.

The concept *race*, as previously defined, refers to any arbitrary classification of human populations utilizing such biological criteria as actual or assumed physiological and genetic differences. The concept *ethnicity*, as here defined, refers to any arbitrary classification of human populations utilizing the bio-cultural criterion of actual or assumed ancestry in conjunction with such socio-cultural criteria as actual or assumed nationality and religion.

The most important criterion underlying the concept of ethnicity is that of common ancestry or peoplehood. Common ancestry, in turn, is a multi-faceted concept implying at least three criteria: biological descent from common ancestors, maintenance of a shared ancestral heritage (culture and social institutions), and attachment to an ancestral territory (homeland). These criteria provide the foundation for the actual or assumed distinctiveness of an ethnic category—a people classified as alike on the basis of ethnicity. The criterion of biological descent from common ancestors underlies actual or assumed physical distinctiveness. When this criterion of ethnicity is emphasized in classification, we may speak of a *racially-defined* ethnic category. The criterion of attachment to an ancestral territory or homeland underlies actual or assumed distinctiveness deriving from national origin. When this criterion of ethnicity is emphasized we may speak of a *nationally-defined* ethnic category. The criterion of maintenance of an ancestral heritage underlies actual or assumed socio-cultural distinctiveness. When this criterion is emphasized we may speak of a *culturally-defined* ethnic category. Frequently, the criterion of ancestral heritage emphasizes one socio-cultural phenomenon such as language or religion.

When the aspect of culture selected for emphasis is language, we may speak of a *linguistically-defined* ethnic category; when it is religion, we may speak of a *religiously-defined* ethnic category.

Although these distinctions are analytically useful, it is important to note that a given ethnic category may be arbitrarily classified on the basis of any one or any combination of these criteria of ethnicity.

An instructive example is provided in the case of the Jewish people.

In the earliest recorded period of Jewish history—some 4,000 years ago—the ethnicity of the people now classified as Jews was expressed in a variety of tribal identifications. Biblical sources (Genesis, 18: 19) suggest that it was with the adoption by the patriarch Abraham of a monotheistic religion, that his tribal followers, and (later) others, were first classified as a religious group, the Hebrews (Genesis, 14: 13). In this period, also, emerged the criterion of ancestral homeland, derived from the Judaic belief in the "promised land" of Israel (Heb. *Eretz Yisrael*)—the land promised to Abraham *and his seed* by virtue of a Divine Covenant (Genesis, 15: 18-19). From this time, the religious self-definition of Jews was associated with this territorial referent.

From the time of the destruction of Jerusalem by the Romans in A.D. 70 and the virtually complete dispersion of the Jews from Palestine by the sixth and seventh centuries A.D. the "promised land" criterion of ethnicity provided, for some Jews, a strong focus for their national self-definition, a focus which, in the nineteenth century, led to political Zionism—a movement to secure the return of the Jews to the "promised land". Other Jews chose to classify themselves as Internationals, Citizens of the World, and to express their Jewish ethnicity only in religiously-defined terms. Still others, rejected their Jewish self-identity and became absorbed into the host nations among whom they lived. During and after the Crusades, when the Jewish people suffered persecution on religiously-defined grounds, the prevailing classification of Jews, by outsiders, was as a distinctive religious group. It was not until 1873, when the racist ideology of anti-Semitism took root in Germany, that the Jewish people were classified, by outsiders (Germans, and later other Europeans) as a distinct (and inferior) race. That this classification did not (and does not) correspond with the biological facts, was of no importance to the people doing the classifying.

This example illustrates that criteria selected for ethnic classification, by insiders and outsiders, are highly arbitrary. Thus they tend to vary with changing social conditions. Moreover, it seems clear that definitions of ethnicity employed by insiders (self-definition) and outsiders (other-definition) may or may not correspond at any given time.

The history of the Jewish people in Canada provides further evidence for the foregoing principles. Many of the earliest Jewish immigrants to Canada came from the countries of Western Europe, where they had lived for some time in relative freedom among their host neighbours. In particular, Jews who migrated to Canada from England in the period from approximately 1760 to 1880, classified themselves, in national terms, as British subjects and considered themselves to be distinctive only on the basis of their religion. This self-definition corresponded, at this time, with the other-definition accorded them by their English-Canadian hosts. The boundary between English-Jew and English-Christian was, in fact, so permeable that many English-Jews intermarried with their hosts and became absorbed into the English-Christian (Canadian) population (Wrong, 1959).

The pre-migration experiences of Eastern European Jews, who formed the bulk of the mass migration of Jews to Canada from approximately 1880 to 1920, was very different from that of their earlier, Western European Jewish counterparts. These Jews came to Canada fleeing pogroms, after a bitter period of forced segregation, harsh legal restrictions on occupation, education and travel, and denial of franchise and citizenship. In the segregated urban ghettoes and small Jewish towns (Heb. *Shtetl*) of Eastern

Europe, they had developed a strong sense of distinctive ethnicity. They considered themselves to be a "people" firmly rooted in a distinctive Jewish religious, linguistic (Hebrew and Yiddish) and culturally-defined ancestral heritage.

Until the formation of the State of Israel in 1948, the Jewish people were not generally classified, by outsiders, as Jews on the basis of national origin. Today, with the Israeli-Arab conflict in the forefront of public consciousness, and with the continuing, overt support given Israeli nationhood by Diaspora Jewry, this classification may, perhaps, be changing. Since 1948, many Jews, in Canada as elsewhere, are increasingly identifying with Israel as their ancestral homeland, their "promised" nation of origin. At the same time, Canadian Jews tend to be highly, nationally identified with Canada as their country of birth and/or citizenship.

It is important, here, to distinguish between *ethnicity* and *citizenship* as bases for nationally-defined sentiments, ties and loyalties. As a criterion of ethnicity, the concept of nationality refers to national/ancestral origins, i.e. actual *or assumed* ancestral territory or homeland. Ethnically-based national identification or nationality may or may not correspond with nationality/national identification based on actual country of birth and/or citizenship. In the case of the Canadian Jewish population in Toronto, the two expressions of nationality appear to be distinct, positively-valued and compatible: Torontonian Jews are reported to be highly nationally-identified with Israel as their ancestral (ethnic) homeland, and with Canada as their country of birth and/or citizenship (Kallen, 1973, Richmond, 1973).

The example of the Jewish people, in the foregoing pages, illustrates an important principle of self- and other definitions of ethnicity. It seems clear, that at any given time, there may be congruence or incongruence not only between self- and other definitions of ethnicity, but also between (varying) self-definitions of ethnicity. Because of the arbitrary nature of ethnic classification, members of a given ethnic category may define themselves as similar/dissimilar to (from) insiders and outsiders utilizing numerous, diverse criteria. This principle allows for a wide range of (both) self- and other definitions of ethnicity at any given time. Moreover, as has already been pointed out, criteria for both self- and other definitions of ethnicity will, inevitably, change in time.

In this part of the book, we emphasize what appears to be a pattern or a trend concerning criteria of ethnicity utilized by people to identify and classify themselves and others. We recognize here that any observed pattern or trend of this kind may not take into account the existence of incongruities through differences in definitions. It is important, therefore, for the reader to keep in mind the fact that some individuals and groups of individuals will probably deviate from the observed pattern at any given time.

ETHNIC CATEGORY AND ETHNIC GROUP

It is important to distinguish clearly between the two concepts, ethnic *category* (or grouping) and ethnic *group*. The former refers to a conceptual or statistical category which may or may not correspond with an actual (empirical) social group. Ethnic categories may be represented empirically by loose, fragmented social aggregates, as in the contemporary case of the Canadian Indian, or by highly cohesive, closely-knit social groups, such as the Hutterites. The Canadian "Indian", as an ethnic category, did not exist prior to contact with Europeans. In pre-contact times, members of various, indigenous tribal and band groupings, such as Cree, Ojibway and Iroquois, categorized themselves and were categorized by others (members of other indigenous groupings) as Cree, Ojibway and Iroquois respectively. But to the European, and (later) the Euro-Canadian, anyone who looked "Indian" was believed to be of common Indian origin or ancestry and was consistently categorized, labelled and treated as an Indian in racially-defined terms. For a long time, the Cree, Ojibway and Iroquois peoples continued to categorize themselves as such, in spite of the fact that they were increasingly categorized by outsiders (Euro-Canadians) as Indian. It was not until very recently, with the emergence of Pan-Indian or Canadian Indian consciousness, that the various peoples categorized as Indians by outsiders began to believe themselves to be of common ancestry and to categorize themselves as ethnically alike on the basis of this belief.

An ethnic category is transformed into a potentially autonomous ethnic group when its members (insiders) categorize themselves as being alike by virtue of common ancestry (rather than being so categorized by outsiders) and interact together so as to develop a common culture and common forms of social organization. All or most members of an ethnic group may or may not occupy a clearly delineated territorial or geographical area. Ethnic group boundaries, separating insiders from outsiders, are primarily *social* rather than geographical.

From the time of the Diaspora, that is, the protracted dispersion of Jews from Palestine, until the creation of the contemporary State of Israel, Jews were a geographically dispersed people, with no empirical territory which they could legitimately claim as their own "homeland". Nevertheless, in many countries they have constituted clearly defined ethnic communities for long periods of time. In Winnipeg, Montreal and Toronto, for example, a large proportion of Canadian Jewish immigrants, from the turn of the twentieth century, have created and maintained residentially concentrated ethnic enclaves where they were and are enabled to interact together so as to perpetuate the religion, culture and social institutions of their ethnic group.

In multi-ethnic societies, such as Canada, residential concentration of members of the same ethnic category at the level of the local community, is an important prerequisite for the transformation from ethnic category to ethnic group. For it is only when people categorized as alike by themselves and/or others, are able to interact continually with one another, that they can develop and maintain their own distinctive culture and social institutions. Once the transformation from ethnic category to ethnic group has occurred, the potential exists for insiders to be able to unite and take concerted action in the interests of their ethnic group as a whole.

ETHNOCENTRISM AND THE DEVELOPMENT OF ETHNIC STEREO-
TYPES

The conceptual distinction between ethnic category and ethnic group is crucial for the understanding of the roles of *ethnocentrism* and *ethnic stereotypes* in inter-ethnic relations. To the degree that distinct ethnic groups maintain their autonomy, each approaches the other from its own ethnocentric perspective. The concept ethnocentrism is virtually self-explanatory. It refers to the ubiquitous tendency of an individual or group to view all the peoples and cultures of the world from the central vantage point of one's own particular ethnic group and, consequently, to evaluate and rank all outsiders in terms of one's own particular cultural standards and values. From an ethnocentric perspective, the traditions, customs, beliefs and practices which make up the culture or way of life of one's own ethnic group are exalted as highest and most natural ("human"). An inevitable consequence of ethnocentrism is the making of invidious comparisons between "we" (insiders) and "they" (outsiders). The greater the differences (actual or assumed) between insiders and outsiders, the lower the evaluation and ranking of outsiders, by insiders.

Ethnocentrism is as old as the record of man. Although commonly attributed to the ancient Hebrews, the idea of a "chosen people" is neither original with them nor unique to them. Anthropological research has revealed the extent to which preliterate peoples refer to their own ethnic groupings as "the people". A great number of names in common use among indigenous peoples, for example "Inuit", the Canadian Eskimo name for themselves, are indigenous terms for "the people" or "human beings", distinguishing members of the ethnic group from outsiders, strangers beyond the pale. Inuit mythology depicts the first man to be created by the "Great Being" as a failure, that is, imperfect; and accordingly to have been cast aside and called

Kadluna (White man). The second man, a perfect human being, was called *Innu* (plural: *Inuit*). The contemporary designation of the Euro-Canadian as *Kadluna* (plural: *Kadlunat*) by the Inuit, contains a further differential assumption, one of economic abundance: Kadlunat signifies not only White people, but "the people who always have plenty" (Hall, 1970, p. 520).

Records of early fur traders and missionaries (Walsh, 1971, p. 41) indicate their surprise upon contact with various indigenous Canadian Indian peoples to discover that the "poor barbarians" held their heads high and regarded themselves as superior to the "White" intruders. It is evident, that upon contact, each ethnic group regarded itself as superior and the outsiders as barbarians.

Ethnocentric evaluations of members of one's own ethnic group and of outsiders are based on shared assumptions as to differences between peoples. Not all kinds of differences are, however, accorded the same social significance. *Assumed* differences between ethnic groups or categories may be physical, cultural or behavioural. Since ethnic groups are believed to consist of people who share a common ancestry, hereditary physical attributes such as skin colour, eye colour, hair colour and texture, the shape of the nose, the thickness of the lips—traits which have, over time been readily observed to differentiate human populations on a global scale—often become important social indicators of ethnicity. Such biologically-defined differences, whether real or fictitious, are important social indicators, but their importance lies only in the use to which they are put: that is, the extent to which they facilitate the ethnic labelling process. Because they may serve to increase the "visibility" of particular categories of people, these (assumed) hereditary physical characteristics enable outsiders to define persons sharing (or believed to share) these attributes as alike by virtue of common ancestry. However, the particular physical traits used as social indicators of ethnicity by outsiders are often *not* characteristics used by insiders to socially differentiate and ethnically define themselves.

Perceived physical differences are only one potential

kind of social indicator of ethnicity. Many cultural and
behavioural traits, such as style of dress, food habits, language, religion, and even certain occupations may come to
be associated, by outsiders, exclusively or predominantly
with a particular ethnic grouping.

The parka and *mukluks* (boots) which have traditionally been associated with the Canadian Inuit are probably
more reliable social indicators of ethnicity to outsiders than
are their particular physical features. Southern Canadians
who have had little or no contact with indigenous peoples
might find it difficult to differentiate between some Indian
and Inuit populations, particularly in the Western Arctic
and Labrador regions, were it not for perceived (traditional) differences in dress, type of dwelling and food
habits.

Where physical traits are not utilized by outsiders as
important social indicators of ethnicity, as in the case of
the Hutterites, cultural and behavioural indices (actual
or assumed) often provide the crucial bases for ethnic
labelling. The Hutterites' high visibility to outsiders stems
largely from their customary practices of social and geographical isolation. Their closed communal colonies, traditional style of dress, and religious practices all contribute
to their assumed uniqueness and hence their high visibility
to outsiders.

All these physical, cultural and behavioural indices,
whether real or fictitious, are important not only because
they facilitate the process of ethnic labelling by outsiders,
but also because they provide the foundation for the creation of ethnic (so-called "racial") stereotypes. *Ethnic
stereotypes* are over-simplified, standardized, and in some
respects exaggerated and distorted images (or caricatures)
applying to an entire ethnic category or group. Ethnic
stereotypes created and/or employed by outsiders to socially define and locate members of a given ethnic category,
tend to emphasize or exaggerate those physical, cultural
and behavioural characteristics (real or fictitious) which
are most dissimilar from those attributed to themselves.
These images are, therefore, distorted because they ignore

the *similarities* between insiders and outsiders as well as the normal range of *individual variation* within the given ethnic category.

The traditional Eskimo stereotype, employed by outsiders (Hughes, 1965, p. 12), depicts all Inuit peoples living year-round in snowhouses (mistakenly referred to as *igloos* (houses), eating raw meat, rubbing noses, swapping wives, leaving female infants and old people out on the ice to die, and wandering about without any sense of time or social order. The label *Eskimo* (raw meat eater) is itself an example of negative ethnic stereotyping, imposed upon the Inuit by outsiders. The stereotypic image, stimulated by the word Eskimo, though based to a limited extent on fact, is distorted, and in many respects, simply fictitious.

Few traditional Inuit groups have ever lived in snowhouses, in fact, this practice has been almost entirely limited to Canadian Inuit groupings from the central and eastern Arctic regions. Moreover, snowhouses are seasonal rather than year-round dwellings. The prevailing ethnic stereotype tends to eclipse not only the diversity among various Inuit groups, but the fact of continuing social change. Most Canadian Inuit today live in permanent settlements and dwell in prefabricated houses with oil heat and electricity. Snowhouses now provide only temporary travel accommodation in the winter months. Nevertheless, southern Canadians continue to envisage all Inuit in terms of the traditional Eskimo stereotype and exhibit disbelief when presented with facts to the contrary.

The tendency of outsiders to evaluate Inuit traditions and practices from their own ethnocentric perspectives has led to misunderstandings about customary practices such as wife exchange and female infanticide. Most Euro-Canadians tend to evaluate these traditional Inuit patterns in terms of their own, that is, Western, Judaeo-Christian standards, and thus deem them immoral and cruel. In fact, such practices were once necessary survival techniques. By facilitating and favouring the survival of the most active and productive members of the group, the male hunters, the perpetuation of the ethnic group as a whole, in a harsh and often hostile Arctic environment, was ensured. Today, with improved economic conditions brought about by government allowances and pensions, these practices have all but disappeared.

The persistence of the traditional Eskimo stereotype may be attributed in part to the relative geographical isolation of the Inuit ethnic grouping from the mainstream of Euro-Canadian society. Most Euro-Canadians simply do not come into direct contact with Inuit peoples. But even where there is repeated contact between ethnic groups, modification of ethnic stereotypes is not likely to occur unless there is a reduction of social distance.

The concept, *social distance*, refers to the degree of social interaction, both quantitative and qualitative, between individuals or groups in contact. Social distance between members of different ethnic categories in contact can be measured in terms of the number and variety of social relationships as well as the degree of intimacy and personal individuality which characterizes the social relationships between insiders and outsiders. Since people tend to act in terms of their own ethnocentric evaluations of themselves and others, social distance in relationships between insiders (*intra-ethnic* relations) tends to be minimized; whereas social distance in relationships between insiders and outsiders (*inter-ethnic* relations) tends to be maximized. When social distance is high, social relationships between members of different ethnic categories tend to be of a categorical or impersonal nature, based on mutual utility. In this context, insiders relate to outsiders in terms of ethnic stereotypes rather than as individual personalities, because most people do not get close enough to outsiders to test the accuracy or inaccuracy of their preconceived, stereotyped notions. On the other hand, when social distance is reduced, and members of different ethnic categories interact more frequently and more informally, social relationships tend to become more intimate and more individualized. In this context, people become increasingly aware of the similarities (rather than the differences) between insiders and outsiders, while at the same time they become more conscious of individual differences among people categorized as outsiders. When this happens, members of the different ethnic categories in contact may come to relate to each other on a close, personal level without reference to ethnic stereotypes, but as social equals and as individual human personalities.

For example: given the increasingly multi-ethnic population composition of the urban-Canadian educational institution, students from many different ethnic categories are being brought, more and more, into direct, continuous, day-to-day contact. To the extent that these young people evaluate students from different ethnic categories, not as individual human beings, but in terms of preconceived ethnic stereotypes, they tend to limit their social relationships with ethnically different students to the formal, educationally-defined activities and pursuits of the school. Thus social distance between students from the various ethnic categories remains high. If however, students begin to perceive fellow students from different ethnic categories as age-mates, sharing common educational, social and recreational interests and problems, these perceived similarities may come to override previous (assumed) ethnic differences, and social distance will accordingly be reduced. When this happens, students may begin to form close, personal friendships with some students from other ethnic categories, in much the same way as they choose their friends from within their own ethnic category. That is, they will perceive not only the similarities between themselves and others, but the individual differences, and they will predicate their friendships on the bases of perceived common interests and individual personality preferences without reference to ethnic stereotypes.

THE FUNCTION OF ETHNIC STEREOTYPES

Ethnic stereotypes serve to reduce the likelihood of first-hand, continuous, informal contact between members of different ethnic categories and thus function to maintain a high level of social distance between the groupings. Each ethnic category remains virtually unknown to the other and an *invisible wall* between them is perpetuated. The invisible wall, separating and isolating the different ethnic groupings is built on common assumptions (real or fictitious, customary or legal, oral or written) concerning "appropriate" behaviour towards members of particular ethnic groupings: certain categories of outsiders are to be avoided at all costs; others may be tolerated "at a distance"; but only members of the category or categories designated as "insiders" are customarily invited to dinner and selected as marriage partners. The ethnic stereotypes underlying the invisible wall between the various ethnic categories thus constitute an integral part of the *boundary-maintaining mechanisms* of the ethnic groups in contact. They are implicit in the ideologies, policies and practices which serve to strengthen ethnic group boundaries by depersonalizing, restricting or totally preventing social interaction between insiders and outsiders, in particular social contexts or spheres of social life.

Historically, in Canadian society, one of the most important vehicles for the perpetuation of negative and often highly erroneous ethnic stereotypes has been provided by written and pictorial accounts of particular ethnic categories contained in children's school textbooks. In their recent study, entitled *Teaching Prejudice* (1971)—a content analysis of social studies textbooks authorized for use in Ontario—McDiarmid and Pratt found that the Canadian Indian, the "non-White" minority most frequently mentioned in social studies textbooks, emerged as the most unfavourable group (*Ibid.* p. 51). An overwhelming number were portrayed, in terms of negative ethnic stereotypes, as primitive, unskilled, aggressive and hostile. Although most Canadian Indians have been wearing Western dress for generations, almost all illustrations depict the Indians either in tribal dress, with males wearing feathers or feathered headdresses, or entirely or semi-naked. In similar vein, descriptions contained in history books provide lavishly detailed (and undoubtedly highly biased) accounts of massacres of "White men" by Indians while (parallel) massacres of Indians by Europeans or Euro-Canadians are either omitted or referred to as "fights" or "battles" (*Ibid.* p. 90). The McDiarmid and Pratt study provides clear evidence to support the authors' contention that both pictorial and written accounts in history and social studies textbooks utilized in Ontario schools, consistently reinforce the negative ethnic stereotype of the Canadian Indian as a fierce and ignorant savage.

"Teaching prejudice", through the continuous reinforcement of prevailing negative ethnic stereotypes, has a marked impact upon the attitudes and behaviour of Canadian students. In the case of Canadian Indians, not only have non-Indian students come to identify Indians as brutal savages complete with feathers, paint, tomahawks and war dances, but many Indian students have themselves come to accept prevailing negative ethnic stereotypes imposed upon them by outsiders (such as: savage, lazy, drunk, or dirty) and have thus tended to develop a highly negative self-definition of ethnicity. Negative Indian stereotypes have consistently served to reinforce attitudes of prejudice and practices of discrimination against Canadian Indians and have thus resulted in a continuing high degree of social distance between Indians and Euro-Canadians both within and outside of the educational system (Hawthorn, 1967, pp. 142, 147).

ETHNIC STEREOTYPES AND THE DEVELOPMENT OF RACIST IDEOLOGIES

Early racist thought, which assumes an inherent inequality between the varieties of mankind, is replete with invidious comparisons between human populations based on prevailing ethnic stereotypes (Rose, 1968, pp. 11-12). In the Old Testament, for example, one of the first recorded instances of prevailing stereotyped notions concerning "Black" ethnic groups is contained in the rhetorical question attributed to the prophet Jeremiah: "Can the Ethiopian change his skin or the leopard his spots?"

Assumed physical differences between ethnic groups were dramatically portrayed in ancient Egyptian wall drawings. Clear distinctions were made between the "red faced" Egyptians and the "lesser" ethnic groups and enemies ("Whites" to the north, "Blacks" to the south, and "Yellow" people to the east).

In ancient Greece, famous scholars such as Aristotle, wrote of "racial" differences from a highly ethnocentric perspective. Aristotle depicted peoples of the north and Europeans as high spirited, but lacking in intelligence; peoples of Asia as intelligent, but lacking in spirit; and the "Hellenic race" that is, his own Greek ethnic group, as both intelligent and high spirited!

Racism, as distinguished from ethnocentrism and early racist thought, represents a modern attempt to give the old idea of inherently inferior and superior stocks or races of man, a scientific justification. In essence, racism attemps to scientifically legitimate prevailing racial stereotypes. A racist ideology or doctrine, as previously defined, is based on the belief that mankind is naturally and permanently divided into a fixed number of separate, "pure" stocks or races. All members of each race are believed to share distinctive physical, cultural and behavioural traits immutably determined by virtue of genetic endowment. Most importantly, the various races of man are believed to be *unequally* endowed with various "human" attributes such as wit, intelligence, morality and so forth: some races (inevitably one's own) are believed to be inherently *superior* to others.

Racist ideologies have repeatedly been demonstrated to be scientifically incorrect, but they persist because they are rooted in emotionally-charged ethnic stereotypes, highly resistant to change, even in the face of contrary facts. Racial myths cannot be dismissed on the basis of lack of evidence, because it is not the findings of biologists in the field of race which determine invidious distinctions and programmes of concerted action. Empirical findings on racial differences are utilized in racist ideologies where they fit, and ignored where they do not. Historically, one of the most outstanding examples of the misuse of biological theories to support racist ideologies is in the writings of the nineteenth century Social Darwinists (Rose, 1968, pp. 36-37). While Darwin's own concern was mainly with evidence of biological evolution, many of his followers (who used his theories as the basis for their own), linked biological and socio-cultural evolution together. While there was certainly not unanimous scientific agreement, many scientists of that time took what they regarded as the superordinate status of the "Whites" as evidence of their superiority in terms of the "survival of the fittest" and they accordingly considered "Blacks" to be degenerate, simpleminded, untamed and uncivilized. "Scientific" racism, which began with the writings of Count de Gobineau (1853), was used to justify the slave system in the United States and to support and justify exploits of European colonialists who took up the so-called "White Man's burden" among indigenous peoples in such distant parts of the world as India, Africa and Canada.

RACIST IDEOLOGIES AND THEIR IMPACT ON CANADIAN IMMIGRATION

Prevailing racist ideologies, predicated on the notion of "White supremacy", clearly influenced early twentieth century Canadian immigration policies and practices, and, concomitantly, helped mould and sustain the emerging Canadian system of ethnic stratification (Porter, 1970, pp. 61-68). Clifford Sifton, the man behind the "progressive" early twentieth century Canadian immigration policy clearly used "reputed" biological qualities as criteria for and against the immigration of particular ethnic groups; for it was precisely such qualities which were believed to fit particular peoples for particular tasks. Thus, such groundless assertions as "climatic unsuitability" were used to justify the exclusion of assumed "biologically inferior" peoples from hot, southern climates (notably Blacks) from immigration to Canada—since it was asserted that these people would not be able to endure the harsh Canadian winters.

Although non-European immigration to Canada still constitutes only a very minor part of the total, the relative proportion has increased in recent years. "Non-White" immigration, however, remains consistently low, making up only four per cent of the total post-World War II immigration into Canada (Richmond, 1970, p. 86). Richmond points out, that until 1962, the Canadian Immigration Act was clearly administered so as to discriminate against "Asian" and "Negro" immigrants. The myth of White supremacy has not only permeated Canadian immigration policy and practice, but has also exerted a continuing influence on the nature of social and ethnic stratification in Canada.

SOCIAL AND ETHNIC STRATIFICATION IN CANADA

Social stratification refers to the evaluation and ranking of social categories, i.e. *categories* of people, rather than *individuals*. The three fundamental dimensions of evaluation for ranking, found within all systems of social stratification are power, privilege and prestige.

Power can be said to relate broadly to the political dimension of social life. The concept, power, refers to the ability of some people to control the life chances of others. The prime social indicator of power, in a modern industrialized society such as Canada, is the attainment of *strategic decision-making positions* within the major social (economic, educational, legal and political) institutions of the society. Through the attainment of these high-ranking positions, members of some social categories are able to make the crucial decisions which affect the life chances (opportunities and rewards) of others.

Privilege can be said to relate broadly to the economic dimension of social life. The concept, privilege, refers to the accumulation and the means of accumulation of the valued goods or resources of a society. Social indicators of privilege, in Canadian society, include wealth, property, income, education and occupation. Sociologists often refer to this dimension of a stratification system as "socio-economic class".

High ranking of particular social categories in terms of power and privilege is (theoretically or ideally) based on personal achievement and is (empirically) indicated by proportionate representation in the elite sphere of *public* life, that is, in positions of wealth and influential/authoritative decision-making within the formal, *secondary* institutions of the society.

Prestige can be said to relate broadly to the inter-personal, informal or *primary*, private sphere of life. The concept, prestige, refers to esteem and/or deference accorded particular categories of people by members of society at large, and especially by the social leaders or "core" elite of the society (Kelner, 1969). The prime social indicator of high ranking in terms of prestige in Canadian society is membership in the private social clubs and gatherings, and participation in the primary social relationships of the social leaders and/or elites of the society.

The particular rank (status) accorded a group on one dimension of stratification (e.g. privilege) may or may not correspond with its ranking on other dimensions (e.g. power or prestige).

In other words, a given group or category may be said to have *status consistency* or *inconsistency*. Of crucial importance, here, is the relative status or position of particular social categories in the *public*, vis-à-vis the *private* spheres of social life. In the public sphere, high ranking may be based on personal *achievement*. In the private sphere however, *ascriptive* characteristics such as ethnicity, religion, family background and "connections" (relatives and friends) may play a much more significant role in determining which social categories will be included as insiders, and which will be excluded as outsiders. A high level of prestige gained through achievement in the public sphere may not be sufficient to ensure a commensurate level of prestige in the private sphere. For members of social categories, who, by virtue of ascriptive characteristics, are excluded from participation in the informal, primary relationships of the social elite, high ranking in terms of prestige is clearly impeded.

MAJORITY AND MINORITY

The concept, *majority* or *dominant group*, refers to the category or categories of people who occupy the highest ranking or superordinate position within the society in terms of power, privilege and prestige. The concept *minority* or *subordinate group*, refers to the category or categories of people who occupy a lower ranking or subordinate position vis-à-vis the majority group. The crucial characteristic of minority group ranking is not numerical strength (many minorities far outdistance the majority in population numbers) but its inferior social position because of which its interests are not equally or effectively represented in the major, public and private social institutions of the society. The concept, minority, is a *relative* term and thus has no social meaning apart from its relation to the concept, majority. Any social scientific study of minority groups must, therefore, always be concerned with majority-minority relations: for it is the majority group which sets the pattern of stratification; determines the initial distribution of life chances and rewards; guarantees the stability of the system, and sustains it.

ETHNIC STRATIFICATION AND THE MAJORITY MODEL

Ethnicity, like religion, language or culture is only one potential criterion upon which a system of social stratification or hierarchical ranking of categories of people, may be constructed. Where ethnicity constitutes an important criterion for social ranking, as in Canada, the society can be said to be ethnically stratified: thus the system of social stratification may be viewed and studied as an ethnic stratification system. In such a system, social evaluation and treatment accorded members of particular minority ethnic groups by the majority depends upon their position at the time within the existing ethnic hierarchy. The position of any minority ethnic group or category is itself based, at least in part, on members' *assumed* physical, cultural and behavioural attributes, *as defined by the majority*. In a theoretically "open class" system, such as Canada, where equality of opportunity is an officially acknowledged ideal, there is a considerable amount of upward and downward social mobility on the part of members of various minority ethnic groupings. The position accorded a particular ethnic minority may thus change over time, depending on the willingness (or unwillingness) of the dominant ethnic group or groups to allow effective participation of minority members in the major social institutions of the society, and on the willingness (or unwillingness) of members of particular ethnic minorities to so participate.

Ethnic group boundaries separating majority and minority ethnic categories and barring equal access to life chances and rewards for ethnic minority members, vary in strength and permeability with the particular ethnic groups or categories in contact. Since the ethnic ranking order is based on the assumptions of the dominant group (or groups), the more a minority ethnic group approximates the majority model, in physical, cultural and behavioural characteristics, the weaker and more permeable the boundaries of the majority; the greater the opportunities for communication between the groups and the greater the chances for upward social mobility of minority ethnic members. Thus those minority ethnic groups whose members (in substantial numbers) physically resemble and share the socio-cultural patterns and values of the majority, and who desire equal participation in majority institutions, tend to move up most quickly in the ethnic hierarchy. On the other hand the less an ethnic minority approximates the majority model, the stronger and more impermeable the majority boundaries; the more restricted the communication between the groups and the more limited the opportunity for social mobility for minority ethnic members.

John Porter's study, *The Vertical Mosaic* (1965), gives evidence that this model of majority or dominant group conformity, is implicit in the Canadian system of ethnic stratification. Represented in the greatest numbers at the top of the Canadian ethnic hierarchy are those ethnic categories most closely resembling the dominant "W.A.S.P." (White, Anglo-Saxon, Protestant) elite, physically, linguistically, culturally and behaviourally: the British groupings (English, Welsh, Scottish and Irish); the other Western Europeans (German, Belgian, Swiss, etc.), and the Northern Europeans (Norwegian, Danish, Swedish, etc.). Represented in the greatest numbers at the bottom of the ethnic hierarchy are those "highly visible" ethnic categories most dissimilar to the majority, the indigenous (so-called "native") peoples: Indians, Inuit and Métis. In the middle ranks are a wide range of ethnic minorities including Jews, Ukrainians, Blacks, Italians, Chinese, Portuguese, etc., most of whom have experienced considerable upward or downward mobility over time, depending on the willingness of the majority to allow them effective participation in its major social institutions, and on their own members' desire to emulate the majority model: that is, to acquire the majority-like characteristics and qualifications necessary for effective participation. More recent studies (Kelner, 1970, and Richmond, 1969), support Porter's observation that there is a tendency for the hierarchical (ethnic) structure to persist because, despite mobility in the middle ranks, the ethnic composition of the top and bottom ranks remains relatively stable.

RACISM AND ETHNIC STRATIFICATION IN CANADA

Within ethnically stratified societies, the different ethnic categories are socially classified, ranked, evaluated and treated in terms of their members' assumed biological, cultural and behavioural characteristics. The particular category with which a person is identified is very important, for the position or ranking of each ethnic group or category determines, to a large extent, its members' life chances: what opportunities will be afforded them, what jobs they will get, where they will live, what schools their children will attend, what kinds of clubs they will be allowed to join, etc. Those at the top of the social hierarchy, the dominant or majority ethnic group or groups in the society, usually have a relative monopoly of the power, privilege and prestige in the society. In order to maintain their position of dominance and control over lower-ranking ethnic groups, they may promote racist ideologies which provide them with an *assumed* moral rationale for customary and/or legal acts of discrimination against subordinate groups. In other words, by clearly defining members of minority ethnic groupings as "inherently inferior", they attempt to justify, legitimize, and perpetuate the existing system of social, economic and political inequality, and, more particularly, their superordinate position within it.

Historically, in Canada, racism towards indigenous peoples has taken the form of paternalistic policies and treatment. The Indian Acts passed by parliament nearly a century ago provide the chief legal source for paternalism towards Canadian Indians. These Acts, dating from 1876 to the present, continue in practice, a policy of wardship initiated by the British to protect a supposedly "childlike" people considered incapable of managing their own affairs. In addition, an even more paternalistic tendency towards protecting Indians *against themselves* is readily discerned in reading these legal documents. (Indian Act—Office Consolidation—1965).

Prior to the Emancipation Act passed by the British parliament in 1833, racism towards "Negroes" or Blacks in Canada was overtly expressed in the institution of slavery. As slaves, Black men and women were advertised and sold on the open market in much the same manner as cattle or home furnishings. They were evaluated and treated as "things" rather than as human beings (Davis and Krauter, 1971, pp. 43-44).

In the early part of this century, Canadians, referring to the Chinese and Japanese peoples of Canada, often spoke of the "Oriental problem" or, in more overtly racist terms, of the "yellow peril". The largest immigration of Chinese to Canada had taken place in the late nineteenth century when labourers were needed to work on the construction of the Canadian Pacific Railway. The Chinese were viewed as a cheap, transitory labour force, to be exploited for particular projects and then sent home. They were not viewed as human beings, worthy of becoming a permanent part of the Canadian population. The fact that a large number of Chinese immigrants did not return to their homeland, but chose to remain permanently in

Canada, constituted the basis of what was later known as the "yellow peril" (Ibid. p. 55).

Racism, in the context of majority-minority relations, is a political tool, wielded by the dominant ethnic group to justify the status quo and rationalize the disabilities to which the minority group is subject. It is clear that the concept of racism, in its most inclusive definition, refers not only to an ideology which proclaims the superiority of one ethnic group over another, but also to actions on the part of one ethnic group which have disadvantageous effects upon another. Thus, within an ethnically stratified society, racism implies the idea of differential power, utilized by the dominant or majority ethnic group(s) to effectively prevent members of ethnic minorities from gaining access to power, privilege and prestige (Yetman and Steele, 1971, p. 362).

A racist belief or doctrine, essentially represents a form of *prejudice*; a racist act or practice represents a form of *discrimination*.

Racial prejudice refers to a set of attitudes or beliefs towards members of particular ethnic categories or groups on the basis of their assumed physical, cultural and/or behavioural characteristics. Attitudes of prejudice may be expressed in diverse forms, from a relatively unconscious aversion to members of a particular ethnic group, to a comprehensive, well-articulated and coherent ideology of racism. It is important that prejudice be clearly distinguished from discrimination: the former refers to attitudes or beliefs, the latter to behaviour. *Racial discrimination* refers to the act or practice or granting or denying members of particular ethnic categories or groups access to life chances (opportunities or rewards) because of their assumed physical, cultural and/or behavioural characteristics (Article I, U.N. International Convention on the Elimination of all Forms of Racial Discrimination). Such discrimination may stem from conscious, personal prejudice. This form of racial discrimination has been termed *individual racism*. Often, however, discrimination does not derive from overt individual prejudice, but rather from the carrying out by an individual of the dictates of others who are prejudiced or of a prejudiced society. This form of racial discrimination has been termed *institutional racism*. Both individual and institutional racism can ultimately be attributed to prejudicial attitudes: either the actor is himself prejudiced, or he conforms to the sanctions of a prejudiced (or assumed prejudiced) reference group. The third and most important form of racial discrimination, long overlooked by scientific investigators in the field of race/ethnic relations, is structural racism. *Structural racism* refers to inequalities rooted in the system-wide operation of a society which exclude substantial numbers of members of particular ethnic categories from significant participation in its major social institutions. The crucial issue here is not that of equal opportunity for those with equal qualifications, but beyond this, the question of the access of members of particular ethnic groups to the very qualifications (skills, resources) required by the majority ethnic group or groups for full participation in the life of the society (*Ibid.* p. 363).

The most blatant form of racist behaviour, and one which most Canadians today would probably vehemently disclaim, is individual racism. The Ontario Human Rights Commission, for example, has dealt with hundreds of cases of discrimination against Blacks and Chinese in employment and housing, but rarely, if ever, does the personnel manager (or realtor) admit to being motivated by personal prejudice. In most cases, the personnel manager (or realtor) placed in a position of hiring (or selling), disclaims personal prejudice as his reason for having refused the member of the ethnic minority the desired job (or home). The grounds for his racist behaviour may indeed have been other than personal prejudice. He may have been carrying out the unwritten policy or "gentlemen's agreement" of his employer (or client) against hiring or selling to members of particular minority ethnic groups such as Blacks and Chinese. If the personnel manager (or realtor) was motivated by overt or conscious personal prejudice his act would be an example of individual racism. If, on the other hand, he bore no personal prejudice towards Blacks or Chinese but was carrying out the dictates or assumed dictates of a prejudiced employer (or client), his act would be an example of institutional racism. In both cases, the *effects* of his action would be the same: the arbitrary denial of equal opportunities for full participation in the major, social institutions of Canadian society to members of ethnic minorities whose qualifications are equal to those of the majority member. Both individual and institutional racism can be ultimately attributed to prejudicial attitudes (overt or covert). If, however, prejudice could be (suddenly) totally eliminated from the system, the structural inequalities rooted in the everyday *impersonal* (that is, *non-intentional*) operation of the ethnic hierarchy would continue to exclude substantial portions of members of some ethnic minorities from full participation in the major institutions of society at large. Because of the existing, unequal distribution of opportunities and rewards, Blacks, as well as Indians, Inuit and most members of highly "visible" ethnic minorities are less likely to possess the *qualifications* required for skilled jobs and the economic resources necessary for purchase of a home.

John Porter's book, *The Vertical Mosaic* (1965), notes that indigenous peoples (Indians, Inuit and Métis) consistently occupy the lowest ranking positions in Canadian society. Historically, a paternalistic attitude based on prevailing racist ideologies, has been employed by the dominant groups (both English and French) to rationalize policies of wardship towards indigenous peoples, which have prevented their full participation in the major, social institutions in the public sphere, and in the primary social relationships (clubs, cliques and gatherings) in the private sphere of the majority society. The result of such policies has been unequal access to power, privilege and prestige. Unequal access to educational and job opportunities has resulted in the fact that Canada's indigenous peoples have the lowest educational levels and the highest unemployment and poverty rates in the society (Porter, 1965). Legal and customary denial or restriction of full franchise and political representation (until recently) has meant that

Canada's indigenous peoples have remained powerless, unable to take concerted action in their own (ethnic group) interests (Davis and Krauter, 1971). Barriers of structural racism in the public realm have been more than matched by parallel blocks in the private sphere of social relationships. Segregationalist restrictions on social participation in the private sphere, by means of special laws or customary policies such as those denying or restricting the purchase and consumption of liquor by indigenous peoples have (until recently) kept indigenous peoples socially separate from the mainstream of the majority society. This has meant that almost all opportunities to acquire the requisite social skills, reduce social distance and break down ethnic group boundaries of prejudice and discrimination, predicated on traditional negative ethnic stereotypes, have been effectively blocked. The crucial issue here is not the equal treatment of Canadians with equal qualifications, but the access of members of some ethnic minorities to the very qualifications (educational, occupational, political, legal and social skills) defined as *required* for full participation in the major social institutions of Canadian society by the majority group(s).

Structural racism, though non-intentional and impersonal in action, has an even greater discriminatory effect for the ethnic minority member who aspires to effective participation in Canadian society than does individual or institutional racism. Because it is so firmly institutionalized, it is extremely difficult to reduce. Anti-discriminatory laws have already reduced the level of overt, individual racism and will probably serve, similarly, to reduce institutional racism, in time. To reduce structural racism, however, would require a willingness on the part of the majority ethnic group(s) to allow a major redistribution of the opportunities and rewards of Canadian society in order to facilitate the attainment of proportionately equal qualifications among members of all (majority and minority) ethnic groups. To eliminate structural racism would require that ethnicity no longer constitute a criterion for social stratification in Canada.

Chapter 7

Origin and Development
of Ethnic Stratification

PREREQUISITES

Despite ethnic differences between coexisting populations in the same region, majority-minority relations do not develop until one group imposes its will on another. When distinct, autonomous groups come into continued first-hand contact, a system of ethnic stratification will generally follow given three conditions: a. a sufficient degree of ethnocentrism; b. competition for scarce, mutually valued resources and c. differential power (Noel, 1971, pp. 32-41).

Without a sufficient level of ethnocentrism, social distance between the people in contact would be minimized, the invisible wall would not develop, and competition would not be specifically structured along *ethnic* lines. Without competition for scarce, mutually valued resources, there would be no motivation or rationale for establishing the ethnic hierarchy. Without superior power it would be impossible for any one group to become dominant and impose its will and standards (and eventually its laws and institutions) upon the other(s) (*Ibid*. p. 40).

Once groups aligned on the basis of perceived or assumed ethnic differences begin to compete against one another, the most important variable in determining which group will emerge as dominant is differential power. Power may derive from the superior size, weapons, property, economic resources, technology, education, skills, customary or scientific knowledge of a group; but whatever its basis or bases, superior power is crucial not only to the establishment of a system of ethnic stratification, but also to its maintenance and development.

Competition between distinct ethnic groups for scarce, mutually valued resources may take place in many contexts, such as war, territorial expansion or migration. Over time, competition leads to an unequal distribution and control of resources, with the more powerful group emerging as dominant. These initial, distributive patterns once established are continually maintained through the exercise of control of society's major, social institutions by the dominant group. The majority ethnic group confers upon its own culture, social institutions and laws the status of societal-wide norms and requires conformity to its social, cultural and legal standards on the part of all ethnic groups. Eventually, prestige becomes associated with control of the society's major resources and social institutions. Thus the dominant group becomes vested with a relative monopoly of power, privilege, and prestige.

The development of the contemporary system of ethnic stratification in Canada began with contact between European intruders (English and French) and indigenous peoples (Indians and Inuit) in a context of European territorial expansion. Initially, the superior power of the European ethnic groups derived from their possession of firearms, as well as their (recognized) superior economic and technological skills and resources. Competition between the ethnic groups in contact resulted in the unequal distribution of land and natural resources with the best, potentially most productive areas taken by the more powerful European ethnic groups.

Treaties between the dominant English group and various indigenous Indian populations resulted in the encapsulation of large numbers of Indian peoples, from many different band and tribal groupings on clearly bounded reservations, often located in the more isolated and less productive areas of Canada. From the beginning, the European conquerors and settlers acquired not only the best Canadian lands, but by far the greatest proportion of this new territory.

Initially, contact between Europeans and Inuit populations was sporadic and limited to economic interaction between the indigenous peoples of the Far North and the whalers or fur traders. The Inuit, living in remote Arctic areas, rarely came into continuous contact with Europeans until the nineteenth century, as the lands on which they lived were not generally considered to be desirable for European habitation nor (potentially) valuable in terms of natural resources other than fur-bearing animals. Traditionally, Inuit people moved in small bands within a fixed radius and rarely tied themselves down to definite localities. Their nomadic and semi-nomadic patterns were predicated on the migratory movements of their animal resources (fish, seal and caribou). Today, most Canadian Inuit live in permanent settlements—selected, designed and controlled by the dominant Euro-Canadian. Initially, Europeans chose the sites which were readily accessible by sea, possessed safe anchorages and were located in areas of sufficient population to be profitable to the fur trader and missionary. These early outpost service settlements —serving the dispersed Inuit camp communities of the region—gradually expanded their spheres of Euro-Canadian institutional control to include not only fur-trading posts and missions, but also R.C.M.P. stations, nursing stations, schools and government administrative centres. Later, with the implementation by the federal government of a large-scale rental housing scheme for the Inuit (after 1965), the outposts became (from the Euro-Canadian point of view) the "natural" choice for the location of permanent Inuit settlements. Frequently, however, the animal resources of the permanent settlement locality have not been sufficient to provide food to support the Inuit population for more than a short time. Thus the Inuit have come to rely increasingly on European food since their movement into permanent settlements (Vanstone, 1971, p. 11).

Because of the initial decision as to distribution of land and resources on the part of the dominant ethnic group(s), Inuit, like Indians, have become more and more dependent upon the whims of the Euro-Canadians for their survival. The important point here is that the initial decision as to allocation of land for both residence and economic exploitation lay with the most powerful ethnic group in contact, and these initial distributive patterns, once established, were perpetuated through the continuing exercise of institutional control by the Euro-Canadian majority.

MAINTENANCE OF MAJORITY CONTROL

Following Confederation, the British ethnic group became the dominant or majority ethnic group at the national level in Canadian society. Although Confederation gave English and French Canadians equal status as the (mythical) two "founding races", English Canadians have increasingly assumed institutional control (culturally, linguistically, and economically) outside of the province of Quebec. As the dominant (national) group, English Canadians have, from the beginning, exercised control of (federal) immigration policies, responsible for determining which ethnic groups would be allowed into Canada, where they would settle, what jobs they could assume, and what ranking and social position would be accorded them within the existing system of ethnic stratification. In order to ensure the dominance of the English majority culture and social institutions, and thus to maintain their dominant position, the English Canadians accorded "preferred status" to linguistically, culturally and socially similar immigrants from the British Isles and northern and western Europe. Less preferred ethnic groups assumed an "entrance status" which implied lower-level occupational roles and social position (Porter, 1965, pp. 63-64).

Changes in immigration policies are indicative of the

willingness (or unwillingness) of the dominant group, under changing social conditions, to allow entrance of ethnic groups highly dissimilar to the majority model.

Richmond (1970, p. 86) points out that until 1962, the Canadian Immigration Act was administered so as to clearly discriminate against non-Europeans and especially "non-White" immigration. Immigrants from Britain, northern and western Europe and "White" immigrants from the Commonwealth countries had preferred status; those from eastern, central and southern Europe were in a secondary position, and those from "Third World" countries had lowest priority.

With continued immigration from Britain and northern and western Europe, the dominant English ethnic group absorbed increasing numbers of these physically, linguistically and culturally similar people within its institutions. Thus the majority group broadened from English Canadian to "Euro-Canadian" (that is, north-west European-Canadian) in ethnic composition. Since 1967, and the new immigration policy based on the points system, "non-White" immigrants with high-level educational and occupational qualifications are, theoretically, admissible without discrimination. However, the traditional emphasis upon active recruitment of immigrants from Britain and northern and western Europe in contrast to Asia, Africa and Central and South America, still acts to favour immigration of ethnic groups most like the majority. In addition, after 1962, the majority of English-speaking immigrants from Britain and northern and western Europe possessed high levels of educational and occupational skills and thus quickly moved into high-ranking positions within the existing ethnic hierarchy. In contrast, most non-English speaking immigrants from southern European countries such as Italy, Greece and Portugal, had little or no education and few requisite occupational skills. Accordingly, they were allocated low-ranking jobs and inferior social positions within the Canadian ethnic hierarchy. Despite the fact that almost one-third of Canada's population (1971 Census, 28.7 per cent) is of French ethnic origin, comparatively few of the post-war immigrants have become linguistically or culturally integrated into the French-Canadian ethnic grouping. Thus the traditional pattern of English-speaking, Euro-Canadian dominance has been retained (Richmond, 1970, pp. 87-90).

Changes in Canadian immigration laws have been largely responsible for altering the ethnic composition of the Canadian system of stratification. The shift has been from a predominantly bi-ethnic (English-French) to a multi-ethnic *content*. However, the manner in which these laws have been administered has reinforced rather than changed the *form* of the established ethnic hierarchy. Despite the fact of constant mobility of both older and newer immigrant groups within the intermediate ranks of the system, the superordinate position of the English-speaking, Euro-Canadian majority, as well as the lowly position of the visibly different ethnic minorities, especially the indigenous peoples (Indians, Inuit and Métis) is virtually unchanged.

Initially, the determining factor in majority-minority relations is differential power. However, once a system of ethnic stratification is well established, prestige becomes of major importance in social relationships between members of majority and minority ethnic categories. Despite rapid and extensive upward mobility within the public sphere of secondary social institutions, entrance into the private sphere of primary social institutions of the dominant ethnic group(s) is far more difficult. Economic and political success in the public sphere, do not guarantee a commensurate level of prestige and social acceptance in the private sphere, for members of ethnic minorities. Kelner's recent study (1969) indicates, that in Toronto, despite increased access of members of ethnic minorities, particularly Jews and Italians, to strategic positions of political and economic influence, entrance into the private clubs and gatherings of the dominant, British elite has been no more than "token". However, the willingness or unwillingness of minority ethnics to penetrate majority social institutions in the private sphere must be taken into account here. Kelner points out, for example, that, *in Toronto*, many members of both the Jewish and Italian ethnic minorities tend to voluntarily restrict primary social relationships in the private sphere to ethnic insiders, i.e. to fellow Jews and Italians respectively. Thus they express little or no desire to penetrate the private social world of the majority elite.

ETHNIC GROUP BOUNDARIES

Any system of ethnic stratification is dynamic: potentiality for increased or decreased communication between the peoples in contact may emanate from either or both majority and minority ethnic groups. A (given) majority ethnic group may vary from time to time and place to place in the degree to which it allows penetration of ethnic minorities into its major social institutions. Similarly, ethnic minorities may vary in the degree to which their members *desire to* participate in the various social institutions of the majority society, as well as the degree to which they aspire to majority *ethnic* status.

The degree of permeability or impermeability of the invisible wall between ethnic majority and minority is largely a function of the nature of ethnic group boundaries. *Ethnic group boundaries* essentially represent the social rather than the geographical or territorial boundaries of the group: they are the social and cultural indicators of ethnicity (ethnic group ascription and identification) employed by insiders to socially define and locate themselves.

From a *subjective* point of view, it is the boundary which defines the ethnic group, rather than the objective characteristics of the people and culture enclosed within it (Barth, 1969, pp. 14-15). Barth points out that it makes little or no difference how dissimilar members may be, physically, culturally or behaviourally if they say they are "Jewish" or "Black" in contrast to "English", "French" or more broadly "Canadian" they are willing to be evaluated and treated as Jewish or Black and not Anglo-Franco—or Euro-Canadian. In other words, they consciously declare their primary identification with and allegiance to the people and culture of the "Jewish" or "Black" ethnic grouping.

Two opposing forces are constantly at work on ethnic group boundaries: a. centripetal or "pull" forces, keeping the member strongly, positively identified with the ethnic group and inducing him to remain within it (and) b. centrifugal or "push" forces, separating the member from the ethnic group and attracting or pushing him out of it (Lewin, 1948, pp. 192-195). Put simply, the nature of any ethnic group boundary is the result of a particular combination of push and pull forces. In the case of the dominant or majority ethnic group, centripetal or pull forces generally work efficiently to keep most members within the fold. In any system of ethnic stratification members of the dominant ethnic group are most likely to find their needs and goals furthered by group membership. Dominant group members thus tend to develop a positive orientation towards retaining group membership. Members of ethnic minorities, on the other hand, are far more likely to be hampered by group belongingness. Whether or not members of ethnic minorities desire and attempt to shift their primary focus of identification and allegiance from minority to majority ethnic groups depends upon the degree to which they perceive (or assume) that their needs and goals can best be met by minority vis-à-vis majority ethnic membership.

To the socially mobile, the minority ethnic group is often viewed as a source of frustration, preventing access to valued majority goals. To the extent that minority ethnic members feel that their desires for upward mobility, and/or aspirations toward majority *ethnic* status are threatened by being identified with a particular ethnic minority, they can be said to be *negatively* identified with their ethnic category. Negatively identified members of ethnic minorities tend to reject the social indicators of ethnicity employed by outsiders and insiders to identify their ethnic category, and eagerly co-opt the social and cultural characteristics and life styles of the majority in order to penetrate the social institutions of the majority society and to gain entrance into (membership in) the dominant ethnic group. However, the ethnic group boundary erected by the majority may serve to severely limit or entirely prevent penetration by minority ethnics. Thus, some minority ethnic group members, who identify primarily with the majority group and aspire to majority ethnic status, are, nevertheless, prevented from leaving their own group. They are kept within the fold by boundaries isolating them from without, ethnic group boundaries erected by the majority. The greater the number of members having a negative identity, the more difficult the effective organization of the ethnic group becomes. The organization of minority ethnic groups held together only or mainly by outside pressures (such as expressed attitudes of prejudice or acts of discrimination by majority members) is characteristically weak. Such groups lack unity of purpose and tend, as a result, to become easily fragmented or factionalized within. On the other hand, in ethnic minorities where substantial numbers of members are strongly, positively identified with their own ethnic group, the group is more likely to be effectively organized, cohesive and strong.

Historically, the persistence of negative ethnic identity among Canada's Black population appears to have provided the major block to the development of effective leadership and organization within the Black ethnic category (Winks, 1971, pp. 95-105). Marked differences among the people categorized by Euro-Canadians as "Black", in country of origin, period of immigration, regional settlement patterns, cultural and educational background and skills, all contributed to the development of internal segmentation and differential class and status rankings within the Black ethnic category. People categorized as Black by the Euro-Canadian majority, include the descendants of fugitive slaves from the United States, highly-educated West Indians and African exchange students, often from traditional, indigenous African nobility. Compounding these objectively-based internal schisms within the Black grouping, is the persistent fact of high levels of prejudice and discrimination against Blacks on the part of the Canadian majority. This strong boundary erected by the dominant ethnic group(s) continues to effectively bar most Blacks from gaining access to high-ranking social positions within Canadian society.

Continually discriminated against on the arbitrary, racially-defined criteria of skin colour and physical features, and divided amongst themselves, many Blacks in Canada have developed a strongly negative Black identity. Until the recent West Indian migration in the late 1960's, the few Blacks who had gained positions of wealth and influence in the majority society had generally done so by "passing"—identifying totally with and co-opting the patterns and goals, appearance and manners of the dominant group—in other words, by rejecting any association with the category "Black". Thus, some Blacks, especially those who could not be readily identified and categorized as Black in terms of skin colour and facial features, have been able to deny their "Blackness", to slough off the negative ethnic label imposed upon them by outsiders, and to cross over the invisible wall from minority to majority ethnic group.

Winks points out that Blacks in Canada have, until very recently, been geographically, historically and socially set against themselves (1971, p. 100). Small in numbers, widely dispersed geographically, and internally factionalized, Black Canadians have, historically, been unwilling to accept the ethnic label imposed upon them by outsiders, yet unable to totally reject the negative ethnic stereotype associated with this label. As a result, the Black ethnic category has been composed largely of negatively identified members, unable to organize, develop effective leadership, or unite in order to take concerted action in the interest of the ethnic grouping as a whole. With the recent immigration to Canada of highly educated and skilled West Indians, this historical picture is changing somewhat, at least in some local Canadian communities, where the Black sub-community has gained considerable numerical strength. In Toronto, for example, a cohesive Black sub-community is developing under articulate young West Indian leadership. The proliferation of local Black organizations and newspapers gives evidence of a growing sense of positive Black consciousness and identity, especially among the younger generation (*Toronto Star*, 1972).

THE DEVELOPMENT OF ETHNIC IDENTITY:
SUBJECTIVE INDICES OF ETHNICITY

A minority ethnic category may consist, initially, of an unorganized aggregate of persons, or (as in the case of Blacks in Canada) various dispersed, fragmented groupings—defined, classified and treated in like manner by the majority. It is only when people become consciously aware of the fact that they are evaluated and treated as alike by outsiders, because of assumed common ancestry, that they begin identifying on this *arbitrary* basis. In many cases, members of subordinate ethnic groupings do not initially regard themselves as being alike, but a sense of shared ethnic identity gradually emerges from a recognition of their common labelling as "people of a kind" by the majority, because of which they are subject to similar social disabilities. One of the main criteria of minority ethnic group belongingness is this recognition of like, differential and discriminatory treatment based on like evaluation and labelling by the majority: what Kurt Lewin has termed "interdependence of fate".

Once people *categorize themselves* as members of a particular ethnic category in contrast to being so classified by the majority, they have developed the potential to transform themselves from a loose, ethnic aggregate to an organized ethnic group capable of concerted action. For the definitive characteristic of an ethnic group is the fact that it is a category of ascription and identification by its members themselves, and thus is capable of organizing interaction between people. The essential prerequisite for the effective internal organization and integration of any ethnic group is the development of a strong sense of ethnic identity on the part of its members, based on an awareness and feeling of "consciousness of kind".

The Canadian Indian leader, Harold Cardinal, strongly

contends that the "problem of Indian identity" in Canada is one of self-definition rather than legal definition (Cardinal, 1971, pp. 138-143). According to the Indian Act, all persons registered or entitled to be registered as Indian pursuant to this Act are *legally* defined as Canadian Indians. This category of legal or "status" Indians includes both Indians whose ancestors signed treaties with the British Crown ("Treaty Indians"), and those whose ancestors did not sign treaties but who chose, under the Indian Act, to have legal Indian status and had their names registered on band lists with the Department of Indian Affairs ("Registered Indians"). However, there are probably as many (around 250,000) non-status Indians as status Indians in Canada today. The category of non-status Indians includes both those people of Indian ancestry and those of mixed (Indian and European or Euro-Canadian) ancestry, or Métis, who do not have legal Indian status. Members of this category of Indians theoretically have the same legal status as Euro-Canadian citizens of Canada. But, Cardinal points out, although non-status Indians and Métis are not legally defined as Indians, they are consistently evaluated and treated as Indians by Euro-Canadians; they are continually discriminated against on the basis of so-called "race". Moreover, many of these people, especially the younger generation, *define themselves ethnically* as Indians. An increasing number are also coming to desire legal Indian status. Thus, all the legal definitions of Canadian Indian ethnicity have failed to solve the real *human* problem of Indian ethnic identification.

When Indians from diverse indigenous backgrounds (Cree, Saulteaux, Mohawk, Iroquois, et al.) began to *call themselves* Indians (in contrast to simply being lumped together and labelled as Indians by the Euro-Canadian) they were expressing a developing feeling of "consciousness of kind". For a long time, however, Canadian Indians accepted not only the label "Indian" but the negative stereotype associated with it. Thus the developing Indian identity was for a long time a negative identity. Indians who had left the relative isolation of reserves or rural Canadian communities and had gone to the city, often found themselves socially segregated, pointed out as "lazy" and "drunk" and penalized for being Indian. As a result, they lost pride in their ethnic identity and sought to hide their "Indianness". Those who could, "passed" into the majority ethnic group.

Today, with the emergence of energetic young Indian leaders working to unify Canadian Indians through Pan-Indian organizations and educational programmes, a shift from negative to positive Canadian Indian identity is taking place, particularly among the younger generation. New Indian leaders and educators are emphasizing the positive contributions of traditional (indigenous) Canadian-Indian culture(s) and are thus inculcating pride in their ethnic heritage among Indian students. Young Indians, (according to Cardinal) are now in the process of discovering a common "Canadian Indian" ethnic heritage and identity and of defining themselves in a positive sense as Canadian Indians. It is precisely this positive, Pan-Indian self-definition which Cardinal contends is the crucial prerequisite for co-operation, unification and effective organization of Canadian Indians at the national level.

In summary, the development of ethnic identity can be viewed in terms of *subjective indicators* as occurring in three stages: a. *Recognition of like treatment.* When members of an ethnic category become aware that they are consistently labelled, evaluated and treated in like manner on the basis of assumed common ancestry (real or fictitious) they may begin to identify ethnically on this arbitrary basis. b. *Recognition of interdependence of fate.* When members of an ethnic category become aware of the fact that they are subject to the same social disabilities because of similar ethnic labelling and evaluation by outsiders, they may develop what the sociologist Georg Simmel has termed "unity in defence": they may begin to unite and co-operate in the interest of their ethnic grouping (as a whole) against the "enemy" outsider. c. *Identification as people of a kind.* Consciousness of like ethnic labelling and treatment, and interdependence of fate, leads to consciousness of kind or a sense of people-hood. Consciousness of kind reduces social distance be-tween insiders within the ethnic category, facilitates communication and co-operation between them, and may eventually result in the formation of ethnic organizations to promote the interests of the new ethnic group. Over time, the ethnic group may develop a distinctive culture rooted in a common sense of ancestral origin or peoplehood (real or fictitious).

OBJECTIVE INDICES OF ETHNICITY

When objective indicators are employed, ethnicity can be measured in terms of four variables relating to the internal structure of ethnic communities: a. degree of disparities; b. degree of social distance; c. degree of social organization; and d. degree of social integration.

Degree of Disparities. Disparities refer to the differences between people. Indices or measures of disparities *within* a given ethnic group may include: age and sex ratios, country of birth, period of immigration, socio-economic class, political orientation, life style, and status systems. The latter measure refers to the possibility of coexistence of *alternate* and *parallel* structures, that is, status systems based (respectively) on criteria incongruent or congruent with those utilized by the majority society.

Degree of Social Distance. Social distance refers to the number and quality of social relationships between people. Indices of social distance *within* ethnic groups include: the degree of voluntary residential segregation, the pro-portion of intimate (primary) social relationships with insiders vs. outsiders, the degree of endogamy (intra-ethnic marriage), the degree of ethnocentrism, and the degree of prejudice and discrimination against outsiders. Ethnocentrism and prejudice can be measured in terms of attitudes and beliefs (world view) as well as norms, implicit or explicit, in customary and/or religious pre-scriptions and proscriptions relating to membership in-clusion and exclusion. Discrimination can be measured in terms of practices (acts and behaviour of membership). Ethnocentric and/or prejudiced attitudes, beliefs and norms as well as discriminatory practices based upon them constitute some of the most effective boundary-maintaining mechanisms (centripetal or pull forces) utilized by ethnic group members.

Degree of Social Organization. Social organization refers to the forms of collaboration or collective activity within the ethnic community. Indices of social organization include: the number and variety of ethnic institutions—degree of "institutional completeness" of the ethnic community (Breton, 1971)—the degree of actual participation of members in ethnic institutions, the degree of interdependence of ethnic institutions, the degree of compartmentalization or overlapping of membership in ethnic institutions, and the degree of use of distinctive communication channels such as ethnic newspapers and mass media, especially in the original (ancestral) ethnic language.

Degree of Social Integration. Social integration refers to the solidarity or cohesiveness of the ethnic group. Indices of social integration include: the degree of congruence of values, interests, goals and loyalties of members; the strength of distinctive ethnic sanctions—especially those of religion; the effectiveness of community mechanisms of social control; the degree of continuity and congruence of the ethnic socialization process; the number and variety of spheres within which concerted action is taken, and the nature of minority ethnic leadership—the degree to which ethnic leaders are "self-styled" spokesmen, representative of particular factions, or representative of the ethnic community as a unified whole.

In order to illustrate these principles, the example of the Canadian Netsilik, an Inuit people, may be instructive. Historically, among the most highly identified Canadian ethnic groups, with clearly defined, strong, ethnic group boundaries, were the tribal or band groupings of indigenous peoples, Indians and Inuit. In the pre-contact period, of all the Inuit populations, the Netsilik or "People of the Seal" (Balikci, 1970) are reported to have exhibited the highest degree of social distance towards outsiders. The Netsilik were nomadic hunters who lived in small bands, each identified with the particular region where its habitual hunting grounds were located. A man born and raised in a given band was identified with it for the rest of his life, even if he emigrated and settled within another Netsilik band. This latter practice, however, rarely occurred because of the Netsilik people's overt suspicion and distrust of "strangers"—people (including other Netsilik bands) outside of one's own local grouping. This high degree of social distance towards outsiders, was probably largely responsible for the Netsilik custom of endogamous first-cousin marriage within the local band.

The Netsilik Eskimos, living in one of the harshest areas of the high eastern Arctic, were able to survive in this cold, desert environment only because of their efficient technology and highly co-operative forms of social organization. The extended family grouping, which provided the framework for subsistence activities (hunting and fishing) was a vitally important kinship unit. Beyond collaboration based on kinship bonds, however, the Netsilik recognized the necessity to co-operate more widely in subsistence activities and food distribution in order to ensure survival of the ethnic group as a whole. The largest sphere of collaboration was in the winter camps where several extended families spent the winter together in order to co-operate in seal hunting. Independent of kinship ties and the obvious need to collaborate in subsistence activities, the Netsilik developed numerous formal and informal dyadic relationships or partnerships such as male song-writing and/or wrestling partnerships and related wife-exchange practices, the overall function of which was to more closely relate generally unrelated people and to increase social cohesion both within a camp and between distant camps.

All these collaborative aspects of traditional Netsilik culture and social organization were centrally related to the problem of survival of the ethnic group as a whole in an extremely hostile environment. Survival of the ethnic unit depended on the primary loyalty of each individual to the group as a whole and the active co-operation of every able-bodied member in all spheres of social life. All decisions affecting the entire community were reached through a general consensus of all adult members. The traditional "Shaman" or religious leader, was often the (unofficial) political leader and was one of the most influential integrating forces in the community, bringing supernatural sanctions to bear on any major form of individual deviation from community interests. In all, the traditional Netsilik ethnic group was highly and positively ethnically identified, tightly organized and integrated, and clearly delineated by strong ethnic group boundaries from all outsiders.

Traditional, tribal forms of ethnic identity among Canada's indigenous peoples were closely associated with both a particular people and a particular territory. Strong ethnic group boundaries were maintained through the continued social and geographical isolation of the ethnic unit. Following contact, both cultural and territorial shifts occurred resulting in considerable social dislocation and problems of ethnic identity among indigenous peoples. When nomadic and semi-nomadic populations were moved into permanent reservations (Indians) or settlements (Inuit), in some instances people from diverse indigenous ethnic groupings were brought together, and in all cases former ethnic group boundaries were altered. Problems of ethnic identity were intensified by internal factionalism which arose within both Indian and Inuit communities: generational conflict; tradition-oriented as opposed to Euro-Canadian oriented sectors and leaders; socio-economic class conflict arising from growing differences in education, occupation and wealth. On a broader scale, the question of ethnic identity raised conflicts between traditional, band or tribal group loyalties as opposed to growing common interests and concerns of particular reservations or settlements, again as opposed to national, Pan-Indian or Inuit interests and loyalties. Until the recent (1971) funding of national organizations for indigenous peoples by the federal government, the relative isolation of many Indian reserves and communities and most Inuit camps

and settlements, compounded by growing problems of
ethnic identity, served to prevent Canadian Indian and
Inuit peoples from uniting on a national scale as Canadian
Indians or Inuit respectively, in order to take concerted
action in the interests of their national ethnic group.
Although it is too early to assess clearly the political thrust
of the newly created national organizations of "native
peoples"—the National Indian Brotherhood (Registered
and Treaty Indians); the Native Council of Canada (non-
status Indians and Métis); and the Inuit Tapirisat (National Eskimo Brotherhood)—some indication of their
potential viability is already evidenced in the proliferation
of recent claims for "just" settlement of (treaty and
aboriginal) land rights, now emanating from these organizations.

CHARTER GROUP STATUS AND ETHNICITY

Ethnic groups which consider themselves to be the
charter members of a society have a special basis for unity.
A "charter group" is one whose institutions provide the
basic structural framework for the society, and whose
members believe themselves to be the "original" inhabitants of an area into which other people have migrated.
This (latter) unquestioned assumption may or may not
correspond with the empirical facts. In Canada, for example, both the English and French groups consider
themselves to be the charter members of Canadian society.
Empirically, of course, Canadian Indians and Inuit occupied the territory long before either so-called charter
group arrived. Nevertheless, the question of charter group
status has an important bearing on inter-ethnic relations
in Canada, for charter member groups, such as the English
and French, often tend to believe themselves to be the
people who "really" belong in the area; others are conceived of as either guests or unwanted intruders.

The Canadian assumption of two charter or founding
ethnic groups lies at the basis of some of the contemporary
problems between English- and French-speaking Canadians; for, since Confederation, only the English have,
(culturally, linguistically and economically,) retained

their charter group status at the national level. In the early days, the dominance of the English majority group was already evident in the preferential status given English and (later) British immigrants. The French looked with great suspicion on the large number of British immigrants entering Canada at the beginning of the twentieth century, and soon became aware that non-British immigrants tended to become English-speaking and adopt the English way of life rather than the French. As *"Les Canadiens"* (the early French-Canadian term of reference) felt more and more threatened by the English-speaking majority they increasingly emphasized their linguistic and cultural differences in order to preserve their ethnic identity. They took on the adjective "French" (French Canadian) and proudly pointed to their high rate of natural increase, which, in answer to the high rate of British immigration they viewed as "the revenge of the cradle" (Porter, 1965, pp. 60-61).

However, the strong persistence of ethnic identity among French Canadians has been facilitated most by the fact, that as a "founding people", they have, at the provincial level, been accorded a high degree of political and religious autonomy within their own "territory". In the province of Quebec, the historical dominance of French-Catholic socio-political and religious institutions has served to perpetuate the French language and culture, despite the gradual encroachment (and eventual domination) of English-speaking, Canadian and American-controlled economic institutions within the province, especially in the twentieth century. French Canadians outside of Quebec have, on the other hand, experienced a far greater loss of both the linguistic and cultural bases for their ethnic identity (Joy, 1972). In Quebec, the alleged charter group status of French Canadians has enabled Quebecers, in an historical environment of territorial segregation, numerical strength, and population concentration, to become and remain largely institutionally complete and thus retain their language and culture to a degree far greater than most non-charter ethnic groups in Canada.

Chapter 8

The Persistence of Systems
of Ethnic Stratification

When a system of ethnic stratification has become institutionalized, established and legitimated through custom and/or law, it becomes a moral order. There is a high degree of consensus regarding "place"—the position of the various ethnic categories within the overall hierarchy. Most members of ethnic groupings know their place, and stay in their place, whether high or low. In other words, the invisible wall, separating and isolating the various ethnic groups, is maintained through consensus. This does not mean that members of minority ethnic groups necessarily accept the inferior evaluation imposed upon them by the dominant ethnic group. They often view themselves as superior and may even view the dominant group as "barbarian" oppressors. The important point is that they accept their subordinate position and comply with whatever obligations and expectations go along with it. They make no attempt to change their position within the system of ethnic stratification or to overthrow the system itself. As long as there is consensus, direct competition between members of different ethnic categories is minimized, as people tend to compete largely within their own ethnic category for jobs, homes, recognition and mates.

Contemporary economic disparities between alleged English and French charter groups in Canadian society have derived largely from a long-term consensus as to "place" and the resultant prevention of economic competition between the two ethnic groups (Smiley, 1972, p. 145). Traditionally, in Quebec, French-Canadian society was rooted in a very conservative, rural, agricultural ideal, closely linked with the Catholic Church and parish. In keeping with this religiously-defined ideal, the French-Canadian farmer was expected to place a primary emphasis on large, close-knit families, and a de-emphasis on material values. Customary inheritance practices among French-Canadian farmers ensured that one son in each family inherited his father's farm. Other sons were encouraged to work towards acquiring their own land, or to enter a French-Canadian institution of higher education in preparation for a professional career as doctor, lawyer, accountant or priest. The traditional, religiously-oriented, classical type of education received in French-Canadian schools and universities produced a relatively conservative French-Canadian elite, reluctant to take elaborate risks and content to remain geographically and economically outside of the large-scale, urbanized, industrialized economic system which later developed in Quebec. Most rural families could not afford to provide all their sons with the opportunities for higher education and consequently, increasing numbers of young men left the rural areas to seek jobs in the developing towns. The paucity of urban, industrial centres in Quebec prior to the twentieth century, coupled with the continuing high rate of population growth, resulted in a steady out-migration from the rural farms of Quebec to New England mill towns and New Brunswick lumbering centres where greater economic opportunities were available. This siphoning off of the "extra" young male population served to help the rural, agricultural, economic system—the backbone of traditional French-Canadian society—to remain relatively stable until the twentieth century.

In contrast to the ideal of rural conservatism among

French Canadians, the primary orientation among English Canadians was, from the beginning on "modernization", that is, urbanization and industrialization. English-Canadian society in Ontario and elsewhere became increasingly secular and materialistic in outlook and encouraged a "progressive", secular type of education stressing scientific and technological skills. As an indirect result of these differences in orientation between French- and English-Canadian society, a very different kind of leadership and elite emerged within the two groups. The emergent leaders of French-Canadian society, the new graduates of the academies, engineering and business schools, chose to remain in small French-Canadian towns, opening up local practices or going into local business or industry. English-Canadian leaders, on the other hand, sought to expand their spheres of influence and control beyond the small-scale limitations of the local town and move into the large-scale professional, political and industrial arena of the developing urban centres.

Over time, the high rate of natural increase among French Canadians in Quebec, coupled with the decrease in available farmland, required the migration of increasing numbers of French Canadians to the cities in search of work. In an effort to halt out-migration, Quebec governments sought capital to create jobs so that maintenance of a numerical French-Canadian majority in the province, made possible by the continuing high birth rate, was not counteracted by out-migration.

By the early twentieth century, Quebec had become a strategic location for manufacturing and the French-Canadian government welcomed "foreign" investment by English-speaking, British-Canadian industrialists and capitalists, as it provided increased money and jobs for French Canadians. Large-scale urban industry was introduced by English-speaking Canadians and Americans who did not encourage upward mobility of French-speaking workers. However, despite the lowly jobs and status accorded them by the dominant English-speaking group, French-Canadian labourers, grateful for the economic opportunities provided by these newcomers, accepted the status quo for a long time. English-speaking Canadians looked down on French Canadians whom they viewed as "backward" products of an "inferior" religious and educational system and a "corrupt" government. Moreover, upward mobility within English-speaking Canadian (and later American) owned and controlled industries was geared to the majority language: only English-speaking workers could expect to be groomed and trained for executive positions; French-speaking workers could not move up beyond the position of foreman, where they were expected to deal, in their own language, with their own "kind". (Hughes, 1934).

Even where the work situation was characterized by an absence of (overt) prejudice and discrimination against French Canadians, differential language created barriers to economic mobility for French-speaking workers within English-controlled industry. Access to higher-level managerial and executive positions involving crucial decision-making, was geared to one's ability to argue convincingly, which, in English-controlled industry, meant that one had to be able to clearly articulate and communicate one's ideas *in English*. Moreover, to be "acceptable" at the upper echelons of the economic sphere, involved not only a firm command of the English language, but also a mastery of the intricacies of English usage, vocabulary and "correct" pronunciation—a requirement impossible for all but the unusually linguistically-adept French-speaking Canadian to meet (Keyfitz, 1968, p. 174).

Despite increased formal contacts between English- and French-speaking Canadians within the context of developing urban industries in Quebec, direct competition between members of the different ethnic groups continued to be prevented by overt or covert discriminatory practices in hiring and promotion, employed by the dominant English-speaking group. It was a long time before consensus about place began to break down, and French Canadians in Quebec became highly conscious and resentful of their status as a subordinate (minority) ethnic group within their own territory.

Differences in class and status do not prevent friendly

co-operation between members of majority and minority ethnic groups who must work together, but friendly inter-ethnic relations are generally limited to the domain of formal, public institutions and do not carry over into the informal, private sphere of interaction. Close, personal friendships are usually confined to ethnic insiders.

This dichotomy between public and private spheres of social interaction serves to limit opportunities for economic mobility of members of ethnic minorities, by maintaining a high level of social distance between the categories. For example, Keyfitz (1968, pp. 172-173), writing about relations between English- and French-speaking Quebecers in the early 1960's, points out that the co-operative structure of the work situation in the higher levels of English-speaking industry in Quebec operated, at this time, to inhibit entry of all those whose command of the English language was less than "perfect". Because co-operative activities between fellow members of the "management team" extended far beyond the work situation into the private sphere of family life and social gatherings, criteria for selection of team-mates approximated those used in selecting close friends. For example, the senior employee was expected not only to speak English perfectly, but also to play a good game of golf. Similarly, his wife was expected to have the "appropriate" (i.e. English) linguistic skills and social graces which would enable her to "fit into" the circle of executive wives. Keyfitz argues, from the viewpoint of the link between language and culture, that disparities between languages reflect parallel disparities between values and life styles. This "bundle" of disparities served, in the 1960's, to prevent non- or poor English-speakers, and French-speaking Canadians in particular, from gaining the social acceptance required in order to penetrate the higher ranks of English-speaking industry in Quebec.

Where status discrepancies between majority and minority ethnic groups are consistently reinforced by (majority) racist assumptions predicated on perceived high visibility, the invisible wall between the categories is even more stringently maintained. In the newly developed settlements in the Canadian Arctic, social relationships between Inuit and Euro-Canadians, tend to be highly utilitarian in nature and almost totally limited to the sphere of work.

A study carried out just after the development of a new mining community in the Eastern Arctic, in the late 1950's, revealed that, at this time, the Euro-Canadian company in control of the mine adopted a policy of "protectionism" toward Inuit workers which guaranteed a high level of social distance between Euro-Canadians and Inuit in all spheres of community life. The investigators (Dailey and Dailey, 1961), argue that the paternalistic policy "ensures that the Inuit is trained to be a labourer, but not a full and equal citizen of the community". Decision-making affecting mine and community is a Euro-Canadian prerogative. Inuit with "desirable" Euro-Canadian attributes (hard-working, frugal, punctual and conformist) are employed in low-ranking jobs, as labourers, by the mine. Those who do not readily adjust to the "White man's ways"—who sleep late, malinger, or do not pay attention to orders, are rejected and forced to leave the community. Although Inuit and Euro-Canadians employed at the mine work side by side, inter-ethnic relationships within the broader context of the work situation are largely symbiotic. Inuit and Euro-Canadians neither eat together at the mine nor attend movies together. Even in the work situation there is no crossing of the invisible wall, if for no other reason than a language barrier. Beyond work, most Euro-Canadians have no idea of how the Inuit lives. The Inuit have their separate residential area and sphere of social activities, and the Euro-Canadians have theirs. Only mission personnel are allowed to visit Inuit in their homes. Euro-Canadian personnel employed at the mine, are forbidden to enter the Inuit settlement without special permission. Motivated by a racist fear of miscegenation, Euro-Canadians discourage any indication of "familiarity" on the part of Inuit women and, in several instances, such alleged "undesirables" were forcibly removed from the community. Inuit never visit Euro-Canadians. Only in the case of Inuit women employed as domestics is an Inuit normally present inside a Euro-Canadian home. Inter-ethnic relations are clearly structured along rigidly limited, impersonal, utilitarian lines set down and enforced by the dominant Euro-Canadian group. The paternalistic policy of the Euro-Canadian mine is (purportedly) designed to protect the integrity of the Inuit and their culture, but the Inuit have never been consulted about it. The effect of the continued implementation of this segregationist and discriminatory policy is the limiting and depersonalization of social relationships between the two ethnic groups and the maintaining of a high degree of social distance between them. Maintenance of the invisible wall between the ethnic categories, in turn, preserves the power differential by preventing economic competition between the ethnic groups. High status, decision-making positions at the mine are clearly reserved for the Euro-Canadian.

In most Arctic settlements, contacts between Inuit and Euro-Canadians are not nearly so restricted and economic mobility of the Inuit not so clearly impeded. Nevertheless, this difference is largely one of degree. The typical pattern is one of Euro-Canadian political and economic domin-ance in the public sphere, and of social segregation along ethnic lines in the private sphere.

Although close personal relationships between members of the same ethnic group generally occur largely or entirely within the confines of their particular ethnic enclave, the various ethnic groups within a community are necessarily involved to a greater or lesser extent in the political and socio-economic order of the larger community in which they live. The particular status systems which develop within minority ethnic communities often reflect this involvement in the patterns of the majority society. Min-ority ethnic communities tend to incorporate selected elements from majority social institutions and culture into their minority ethnic counterparts so as to create a trans-formed, hybrid system. To the extent that participation in majority social institutions is desired, but prevented by barriers erected by the dominant group, minority ethnic groups tend to form "parallel structures", status hierarchies emulating those of the dominant group to which they cannot gain access.

The principle of parallel structures (or institutions) implies an acceptance of majority group values and criteria for social stratification. Accordingly, the parallel, minority ethnic status system serves to reinforce the existing, societal-wide system of stratification. Not infrequently, a minority ethnic community, caught between the "push" and "pull" forces of tradition and change, develops more than one kind of status system. Thus, a traditional, *alternate* structure may coexist with a new, *parallel* structure. Members of the ethnic community may become divided along similar lines, into two polar categories, *traditionalists* and *assimilationists*. Traditionalists, operating within the traditional sanctions and criteria of the *alternate* system, will seek to preserve the traditional (ancestral) culture, social institutions and ethnic identity of the group. Assimilationists, operating within the new (majority) sanctions and criteria of the parallel status system, will seek to gain further access to power, privilege and prestige within majority institutions. As part of their strategy for further penetration of majority institutions, they may seek to reduce ethnic visibility by further transforming their parallel institutions along the lines of the majority model.

Although most members fall somewhere in-between these two extremes in orientation, and operate, as the situation demands, within one or the other of the status systems available to them, leadership of the group tends to polarize—if only temporarily—into these two camps. The future of the ethnic community, especially the potentiality for members uniting and taking concerted action in the interests of the ethnic category as a whole, will therefore, depend largely on the outcome of leadership struggles between these factions.

In many contemporary Inuit communities, differential occupation forms the basis of a socio-economic continuum, from a traditional alternate, status system based on full-time hunting and trapping, to a new parallel status system, based on wage work (Vallee, 1968). Traditionally-oriented Inuit, living primarily by hunting and trapping, continue to look to the great hunter as the leader and authority figure "par excellence". Within this traditional, alternate status system, the best hunter in the community continues to provide the model to admire and emulate. In contrast, wage workers pattern themselves after Euro-Canadians, and have developed a new status structure patterned upon the Euro-Canadian model. In this status system, wage work is considered to afford high prestige and work clothes and identification badges, as well as other symbols of Euro-Canadian occupation, are proudly worn whenever possible. At present, the two status systems exist symbiotically, but long-term trends will probably favour wage-work opportunities, and, accordingly, the parallel structure.

MAINTAINING THE STATUS QUO

The general persistence of a system of ethnic stratification depends not only upon the will of its majority group(s), but also upon the tacit compliance of its ethnic minorities. To ensure this necessary compliance of minority members, majority groups often utilize racist ideologies, strategies and policies which are designed to maintain the status quo by strengthening and rigidifying the "invisible wall" (ethnic group boundaries) between majority and minority. Such tactics serve to perpetuate power differentials, prevent economic competition and maintain a high level of social distance between majority and minority ethnic groups. The particular techniques of domination to be discussed here have, historically, been utilized by majority ethnic groups in Canada, as elsewhere, in order to guarantee their ascendency.

Denial of Franchise. In some provinces, and on a federal scale, Chinese, Japanese, Hutterites and Doukhobors have, at one time or another, been denied the vote in Canada. Inuit, as full citizens of Canada, have always had the right to vote in federal elections, but it was not until 1962 that they were given the right to vote in provincial elections as well. Not until 1960 were all status Indians granted the federal vote, and in Quebec, Alberta, New Brunswick and Prince Edward Island they are still disqualified from provincial voting.

Control of Land Ownership and Use. Paternalistic attitudes and policies of the Canadian government towards its indigenous peoples are nowhere more clearly demonstrated than in the absolute control exercised over land ownership and use. Through a long series of unilateral and bilateral agreements between indigenous Indian peoples and the British Crown, Canadian Indian tribal lands passed from Indian control and occupancy to Euro-Canadian control, with specified areas reserved for the exclusive occupancy and use of the Indians. About half of Canada's Indians have treaties with the Crown and/or are entitled to reserve lands and associated benefits. Under the Indian Act, the Minister of Indian Affairs has absolute control in administration and ultimate decision-making concerning Indian reserve lands. Despite the fact that all status Indians (Treaty and Registered Indians) are entitled to reserve lands, there remain numerous unsettled land claims of Canadian Indians. An outstanding case is found in Treaties Eight and Eleven, where the government has not (as yet) compensated the Indians for failure to set up reserves in the Northwest Territories.

Non-status Indians, Métis and Inuit can make no legal claim with regard to their aboriginal (ancestral) territories, which have been appropriated by the Canadian government. Their argument for "aboriginal rights", currently voiced through several organizations of indigenous Canadians, has no recognized basis in Canadian law.

Control of Population Numbers through Limiting Migration (In or Out). Historically, in Canada, the imposition of immigration restrictions has most severely affected those peoples categorized as Orientals and Blacks. Prior to 1953, the inclusion of the notion of "climatic unsuitability" in the Immigration Act, furnished the legal justification for barring people from Third World countries (with presumably hot climates)—notably Blacks. During the nineteenth and early twentieth centuries, the Canadian Immigration Act contained a number of special regulations specifically designed to restrict Chinese and Japanese immigration (Davis and Krauter, 1971, pp. 61-62). In 1886, a federal head tax was imposed on Chinese immigrants entering British Columbia. From 1898 to 1903 the head tax increased from fifty dollars to five-hundred dollars per head. In 1907, Canada entered into a "gentleman's agreement" with the government of Japan restricting Japanese entry to an initial maximum of four-hundred families per year, later reduced to one-hundred and fifty families. No such pact was possible with China; because of the continuing high level of anti-"Oriental" prejudice, especially in British Columbia, Chinese immigration was perceived as a major "problem". By 1903, it was clear to the Canadian government that increases in the Chinese head tax were not serving to deter the flow of purportedly "undesirable" Chinese immigrants. Accordingly, the Canadian parliament passed a new law requiring every "Asian" (except those covered by a special treaty or international agreement) to have two-hundred dollars in his or her possession upon arrival in Canada. When this deterrent proved to be no more successful than the head tax, the government took more drastic measures. In 1923, the Chinese Immigration Act (sometimes colloquially referred to as the "Chinese exclusion act") was passed, forbidding entry of Chinese, under any conditions, until after World War II.

Employment and Wages. The problem of employment among Canada's indigenous peoples is rooted in a self-perpetuating cycle of economic deprivation. Lack of education and training severely hampers job opportunities, and conversely, graduates of special training programmes for indigenous peoples often experience difficulty in finding jobs because of the dearth of employment opportunities on Indian reserves and in small, isolated Inuit settlements. Severe competition from Euro-Canadians plus a high level of discrimination against indigenes in hiring practices, in the more urbanized areas, further restricts job opportunities. The effects on Canadian Indians are evident in the fact that the Indian unemployment rate by 1961, was ten times the national average. In 1961,* the per capita income ($300.00) was reported to be only one-fifth of the national average. Forty-seven per cent of Indian families earned less than one-thousand dollars per year, and forty per cent were existing on the basis of welfare assistance (Davis and Krauter, 1971, p. 16).

Among Canada's immigrant ethnic groups, those peoples categorized as Oriental or Black have, historically, been accorded the highest degree of discrimination in employment and wages (*Ibid.* pp. 65-66). In the nineteenth and early twentieth centuries, Chinese and Japanese, particularly in British Columbia, were subject to severe job discrimination. Denied the franchise, they were excluded from the voting lists and thus from licensed professions. Moreover, they were directly prohibited from other licensed occupations such as the fishing industry, by the customary manipulation of special regulations. They were also denied other positions such as public school teaching. Forced to accept any job at any wage, Chinese and Japanese immigrants became in fact, as in stereotype, "cheap labour". Because they accepted low wages, they were perceived as a threat to prevailing wage standards by the "White" Euro-Canadian workers and by organized labour. As a result, they were excluded from membership in labour unions, and at times were victims of open and devastating racist mob attacks and violence. It was not until the end of World War II, that formal union opposition to Chinese and Japanese immigration in large part disappeared.

Prior to 1833, Black immigrants to Canada were "employed" as slaves. Since that time, Blacks have tended to occupy the very bottom rungs of the urban occupation ladder. Blacks have for a long time been accorded stereotyped occupations such as railway porters (males) and

* 1971 figures not available at present.

household domestics (females). For most Blacks, at present, occupational prospects remain poor due to lack of education and training as well as a continuing high level of job discrimination. Recent, more highly educated and skilled West Indian immigration has changed the picture somewhat, but discrimination in jobs on the basis of skin colour, despite requisite skills, still persists (Davis and Krauter, 1971, p. 47).

Education. Separate and unequal educational opportunities have been largely responsible for the consistent records of low academic achievement as well as high rates of failure and early school dropout among Canadian Indian and Inuit students. Problems of severe age-grade retardation and early school dropout continue to reinforce the stereotype of the insufficiently qualified and therefore jobless young indigenous "transient" (Hawthorn, 1967).

Government responsibility for Indian education was, until the last decade, delegated largely to religious institutions whose leaders (missionaries) stressed religious indoctrination of the alleged "savages" and minimized secular curriculum content so as to fit the educational programme to the (assumed) inferior level of educability of the would-be students. When local, secular schools were set up on Indian reserves, the quality of Indian education did not improve appreciably because of the lack of adequate material resources (buildings, equipment, books, etc.) and the equal lack of adequate human resources (poorly trained and often highly prejudiced teachers).

In the case of Inuit peoples, Canadian government educational policy until the end of World War II was largely one of neglect (Jenness, 1964). Inuit were expected to live off the land and their education was left to a small number of missionaries and mission schools which served only a minute fraction of the indigenous children in the Canadian Arctic. As late as 1944, 93 per cent of Indian and Inuit children in the Western Arctic and MacKenzie Delta Regions were receiving no formal education. It was not until 1947 that the federal government built the first public school for its Arctic peoples. Although there has been a considerable increase in the number of schools and the proportion of school-age children regularly attending these schools in the last two decades, the problems of inadequate school facilities, curriculum and teachers remain particularly acute in the Arctic. The difficulties and high costs involved in transportation of building materials, books, equipment, etc., to the far north, impede adequate programme and curriculum development. In addition, the social isolation and severe climate which characterize Canadian Inuit settlements in the frozen Arctic contribute to a continuing high rate of teacher turnover. As in the case of Indian education, a major block to the Inuit pupils' academic progress lies in the vast cultural and linguistic gap between the Euro-Canadian teacher, curriculum and format, on the one hand, and the Inuit pupils, on the other (Hobart, 1970). Compounding this gap is the lack of communication between Euro-Canadian teachers and Inuit parents. Until less than five years ago, no attempt was made by the Canadian government or by Euro-Canadian educators to take into account the nature of the language, culture or social institutions of the indigenous minority, Indian or Inuit. Moreover, Euro-Canadian educational policies were, in practice, imbued with racist assumptions about the limits of educability of the "natives"—assumptions which tended, eventually, to become self-fulfilling prophecies. Among (status) Indian students, for example, a 94 per cent school dropout rate between grades one and twelve (compared to a national dropout rate of 12 per cent) has been reported by Hawthorn (1967, p. 130). Although no comparative (national) statistics are presently available for Inuit students, the overall level of educational achievement is even lower, due to the much later entrance of Inuit pupils into the Euro-Canadian educational system. Most Canadian Inuit have not, as yet reached the grade nine level.

Separate and unequal education has also been experienced by most Blacks in Canada, until very recently (Davis and Krauter, 1971, p. 45). From 1850 to 1965 Blacks throughout Canada were customarily excluded from the dominant, Euro-Canadian educational structure and relegated to segregated, all-Black schools, typically inadequate in terms of space, facilities and staff. The last segregated Black school in Ontario closed in 1965, but in Nova Scotia, despite the ending of legal educational segregation in 1963, several all-Black schools, serving Black ethnic communities, are still in operation. Where discrimination against Blacks continues to be high, as for example in Nova Scotia, the ending of "de jure" segregation does not guarantee the ending of "de facto" segregation. Although higher-level public education is now (theoretically) open to Blacks throughout Canada, awareness among Blacks (as among Indians and Inuit) of persistent, high levels of discrimination in jobs dampens motivation towards continuing education and encourages early school dropouts. This probably accounts, at least in part, for the fact that 75 per cent of the rural, non-farm Black population and 34 per cent of Blacks living in Halifax were recently reported to have less than a grade seven education (Clairmont and Magill, 1970, p. 59).

Housing. Long decades of neglect of housing demands voiced by Canada's reserve Indians has resulted in the fact that, as recently as 1967, 57 per cent of reserve Indians (in contrast to the national average of 11 per cent) lived in sub-standard housing (Davis and Krauter, 1971, p. 14). Indians off the reserve seem to fare little better; as transients or unskilled workers in the larger cities, most Canadian Indians are reported to live in slum or near slum conditions.

The current problem of housing among the Canadian Inuit is a relatively new phenomenon. It has not therefore received the attention given to the parallel Indian situation. The major movement of Inuit from traditional hunting and trapping camps, where they dwelled in temporary snow-houses or tents (depending on the season) to permanent settlements where they reside in prefabricated housing, followed the implementation of a large-scale housing programme initiated by the federal government in 1965. The housing scheme was predicated on the belief that housing conditions in the traditional Inuit camp communities were a primary cause of the high rate of disease (especially tuberculosis and influenza) and early death among the Inuit population. The relocation of the Inuit in permanent settlements with prefabricated houses has coincided with a decrease in the rates of disease and early death, but this improvement appears to be due as much to the vast improvement of medical services as to the change in housing. The problem of adequate housing remains acute. Expansion of medical services—the building and staffing of nursing stations and hospitals in the Arctic—has resulted in a steady increase in population numbers and family size among the Inuit. Consequently, the demand for more and larger houses for Inuit families far exceeds the present supply. Most Inuit families cannot afford to pay more than a part of the rental cost even of a very small house, and most houses are, therefore, at least partially government subsidized. While Inuit families have become increasingly dependent on government assistance to meet their housing needs, the tremendous cost of both transportation and maintenance of houses in the Arctic, coupled with the continually increasing need for housing has created the current situation in which government supply lags far behind Inuit need and demand. This has produced a growing problem of overcrowding, particularly in the more remote Arctic settlements.

Communications Media. Throughout Canadian history, Canada's indigenous peoples have been depicted in the mass media largely in terms of negative, racial stereotypes. Recent surveys based on childrens' book and textbook accounts of Canadian history as well as newspapers, magazines and television programmes, provide substantial evidence to support the claim put forth by various Canadian Indian and Inuit organizations, that Canada's indigenous peoples are continually portrayed in the mass media in inferior, stereotyped roles (Atnikov, Oleson and McRuer, 1964; D.I.A.N.D., 1969; Elkin, 1972; Indian and Métis Conference, 1964).

Similar complaints of negative ethnic stereotyping are

increasingly voiced by representatives of Canada's Black and Chinese populations. A recent investigation of discrimination in advertising undertaken by the Ontario Human Rights Commission (Elkin, 1972) found that "visibly different" actors and models were rarely selected by their respective employment agencies for jobs in mass-media advertising. Moreover, the few highly visible performers so-employed were not given ordinary roles but were almost exclusively limited to "racially-identified" and stereotyped roles.

Despite Canada's increasingly multi-ethnic character, the primary "Canadian" image portrayed in the mass media remains "White Euro-Canadian". Other minorities, particularly the visibly different, are infrequently represented and when portrayed at all are still largely depicted in terms of inferior, racially-stereotyped roles and images. The manipulation of the mass media so as to reinforce negative, minority ethnic stereotypes remains a powerful technique of dominance wielded—consciously or unconsciously—by the majority group(s) to guarantee its (their) ascendancy.

Persecution and Extermination. Historically, a major reason for immigration to Canada of many ethnic minorities, such as Jews and Hutterites, was to escape persecution in the country (or countries) of emigration. Canada was viewed as a land of freedom and opportunity, where people could live without fear of prejudice and discrimination on religious and/or racially-defined grounds. Although Canada has not, in fact, fully achieved this ideal, the techniques of domination employed by Canadian majority group(s) have tended to be covert rather than overt, and customary rather than legal.

An outstanding exception to this general principle is provided in the case of the deliberate oppression of Japanese-Canadians during World War II. In this particular instance, the combined forces of government policy and public opinion, strongly influenced by the traumatic political climate of the times, vented the fear and anger of the nation upon one ethnic minority. As the national focus for racist persecution, all Japanese Canadians were lumped together, labelled and discriminated against as undesirable enemy aliens.

Within one day of the Japanese attack on Pearl Harbour (December 7, 1941), was an attack on Hong Kong, in which an entire Canadian contingent of two thousand was killed or captured. Fear of imminent Japanese invasion spread rapidly throughout the west coast of Canada and quickly found a target in the large and highly visible Japanese-Canadian population. In British Columbia, the Japanese minority, citizen and non-citizen alike, was immediately designated as a subversive "fifth column" and subjected to a concerted programme of official persecution (Davis and Krauter, 1971, pp. 58-61). Although this programme was primarily enacted under British Columbia provincial policy, the federal government did not interfere and eventually supported it. All persons of Japanese origin were forcibly evacuated from the west-coast defence area and relocated in the interior of Canada where they were subjected to harsh living and working conditions in internment camps. Rigid limits were imposed on the amount of goods evacuees could take with them, and the rest of their belongings had to be disposed of rapidly. As a result, their property was frequently sold at much less than equitable prices.

To ensure a more permanent solution to this alleged "Oriental problem", following the surrender of Japan in 1945 the government ordered the deportation to Japan of all persons of Japanese ancestry. Almost four thousand Japanese Canadians were thus "repatriated" (allegedly voluntarily) prior to the revocation of the deportation order in 1947.

The fact that the deportations were ordered *after* the war and despite any evidence of subversive, pro-Japan activities on the part of ill-treated Japanese-Canadian internees, indicates clearly that the government and the Canadian public were motivated more by anti-Japanese racism than by considerations of wartime security. In contrast to the persecution of the Japanese, little was done to

Canadians of German origin (except the Hutterites) although almost all of Canada's armed forces were engaged against Germany in the war. It seems clear that the racist colour bias which was directed against Japanese did not apply to "White" Germans. During the war period, repressive steps were enacted against other Canadian groups, especially communist, fascist and pacifist organizations but discriminatory measures against the Japanese minority were far harsher than those accorded any other group.

Summary. Techniques of domination are essentially methods and forms of institutional and structural racism. These discriminatory practices have been historically easiest to plan and carry out against highly visible ethnic minorities, especially where skin colour serves as an unalterable social indicator of ethnicity. It is not surprising, therefore, to discover that of all Canada's ethnic minorities, it is the highly visible populations—Indian, Inuit, Japanese, Chinese and Blacks—who have, historically suffered the most severe disabilities because of arbitrary, so-called racial characteristics, over which they have no control.

Neither laws against violating the invisible wall, nor the power to enforce them are too frequently needed in a well-established system of ethnic stratification. As long as the ethnic hierarchy is assumed to be a natural, moral order and remains unquestioned, voices of protest are often branded as immoral and stifled by the very members of ethnic minorities who would benefit from them most. For the perpetuation of social distance between majority and minority ethnic groupings does not depend only on the attitudes and practices of the dominant ethnic group (or groups). To the extent that members of ethnic minorities identify strongly as such, and develop a common culture, unity of purpose, and social organization, processes serving to perpetuate social distance between minority and majority are generated from within the minority community, as well as from without.

In highly identified and closely integrated ethnic minority communities ethnic custom often discourages contact with outsiders, prohibits intermarriage and stifles protest. Ideologies arise which depict the majority group as the "enemy oppressor" responsible for the disabilities suffered by the minority. Such ideologies legitimate the ethnic minority way of life as "just" and "moral" in contrast to the unjust and immoral ways of the majority group(s). To the extent that the ethnic minority is conceived by its members to be superior to the majority, attitudes of prejudice and practices of discrimination against outsiders will persist, and a high level of social distance between minority and majority will be generated from within the minority ethnic group, whether or not it is also generated from without.

Among Canada's ethnic minorities, the Hutterites stand out as a group whose members have consciously chosen to maintain a high level of social distance between themselves and the majority society (Davis and Krauter, 1971, pp. 87-101). The Hutterites or Hutterian Brethren are a religious sect, originally and largely German in ethnicity (on the basis of actual *and assumed* ancestry as well as cultural and linguistic criteria). Since their arrival in Canada in 1899, they have continued to practise a communal, agricultural way of life in Canada's Prairie Provinces. The Hutterites' distinctive world view and form of community organization is rooted in their religion which demands that they isolate themselves, physically and socially, from the "outside world" (which includes all non-Hutterites) and live a simple, frugal, and essentially communal existence. In keeping with this world view, Hutterite communities are small, self-contained, highly self-sufficient, agricultural enclaves voluntarily isolated and segregated from the majority society. A high degree of social distance between the Hutterite group and their Euro-Canadian neighbours is maintained through strict observance of religious rules and customary practices which severely restrict contact between Hutterite and non-Hutterite.

The Hutterite religion is predicated on the belief that man is made to worship God and to strive towards enjoyment of everlasting life after death, rather than enjoyment of temporary, present life on earth. Canadian society, in the Hutterite view, emphasizes enjoyment of present life. This materialistic and sensate emphasis is considered to be dangerous and sinful. Therefore "true believers" (according to Hutterian doctrine) must withdraw, resist the temptations of the allegedly "corrupt" outside world, and isolate themselves from contact with it. To ensure social distance, and especially to prevent intermarriage (prohibited by the Church and punished by excommunication) the few contacts between Hutterites and the majority society are made by carefully selected mediators, such as the preacher, firmly committed to Hutterite values. Geographical as well as social isolation of Hutterian colonies is ensured through the practice of voluntary residential segregation. Each colony purchases a large tract of land (sometimes thousands of acres) isolated from the more highly-populated areas of the region, and strategically houses its community in the middle of the tract. This ensures both social isolation and geographical concentration of the Hutterian population. Continued, close everyday contact among members, increases the degree of social control which can be exercised both by leaders and fellow members of the Hutterian community, wielding sanctions of public opinion against individual deviation from group norms. Within the colonies, the total socialization process is geared to conformity to the religiously-defined community. Religion demands the subordination of the wishes of every individual to the community as a whole. The Hutterian concept of "community" inculcated in every child and adult is as a community in both the material and the spiritual sense.

Like the Japanese, but to a lesser degree, the Hutterites were subjected to discriminatory treatment during World War II because of their *assumed* ethnic connection with enemy powers. In both cases, however, the wartime persecution was not a new phenomenon. Rather, this pattern of discrimination represented an exaggeration of previous patterns, based on the negative evaluation accorded the (assumed) ethnic distinctiveness of these two peoples by the majority Canadian society.

The Hutterites have always attempted to maintain a peaceful and separate existence within their host nations. Because they desire self-sufficiency and maintenance of their religiously-defined distinctiveness, they refrain from active political, legal, educational and social participation within majority Canadian institutions. In fact, they attempt to confine transactions with the "outside world" to those deemed necessary in economic terms. Their refusal to participate more than minimally in the majority communities surrounding them has resulted in the fact that they remain unknown, even to their neighbours. Because they are unknown, yet continue (for unknown, hence "suspicious" reasons) to prosper economically and expand territorially, they are increasingly perceived as a threat by outsiders.

The Hutterites' strategy of encapsulation or withdrawal, their distinctive characteristics, and their continuing economic success have all contributed to their high visibility as an ethnic minority in Canada. Their continuing high visibility has, in turn, encouraged discrimination against them. Accordingly, a high level of social distance between the Hutterites and the majority society has been continually maintained through the employment by both insiders and outsiders of effective boundary-maintaining mechanisms.

Chapter 9

Processes of Ethnic Integration

The concept of integration, in its broadest sense, may be used to refer to all the transactional processes whereby ethnic group members acquire the distinctive cultural characteristics, and penetrate (gain entrance into) the social institutions of an ethnic group to which they do *not* belong. It is important to remember that all processes of integration occurring between different ethnic groupings in contact are essentially two-way transactional processes, whereby members of each grouping may (potentially) seek to acquire some of the cultural characteristics and gain entrance into some of the social institutions of the other. However, the primary direction of integration within an established society tends to be towards the norms and patterns of society at large; and, in an ethnically stratified society such as Canada, the culture and social institutions of society at large are those of the majority ethnic groups(s). For this reason, social scientific enquiry, focussing on ethnic integration within Canadian society, is primarily directed towards the study of processes of integration of ethnic minorities into the majority culture and social institutions.

ACCULTURATION (CULTURAL INTEGRATION)

The concept *acculturation* or cultural integration, may be used in its broadest sense to refer to the process whereby contact between members of different ethnic groups or categories results in the exchange of objects, ideas, customs, skills, behaviour patterns and values between the two groups. This on-going cultural exchange is a two-way process in which each ethnic group selects from the other particular items and attributes which may eventually become absorbed into its own system.

Viewed as a part of a general process of learning, the concept acculturation may be used to refer to the process of learning the cultural values, ideas, behaviour patterns and skills of an ethnic category or group to which one does *not* belong, in much the same way as the concept *socialization* is used to refer to the broad process of learning the cultural ways of the ethnic group or category to which one *does* belong.

Within an established system of ethnic stratification the prime direction of change in the process of acculturation is towards the norms, values and patterns of the majority. Most members of ethnic minorities seek to learn the language, and acquire the cultural patterns (or ways of viewing and doing things) of the majority in order to improve their socio-economic position and life chances. Acculturation, in this context, refers to the process of acquisition, by members of ethnic minorities, not only of the cultural attributes of the majority, but also of the required *level of proficiency* in utilizing these attributes which is deemed necessary for effective participation in the majority social institutions.

The degree of acculturation of a particular individual or ethnic grouping can be measured in terms of: a. The degree to which one has acquired the cultural attributes (or ways of viewing and doing things) of a group other than the one to which one belongs; b. the degree to which one has reached a level of proficiency in utilizing these acquired cultural attributes commensurate with that of people socialized, from birth or early childhood, into that culture.

ASSIMILATION (STRUCTURAL INTEGRATION)

In its broadest sense, the concept assimilation (structural integration) may be used to refer to the process of penetration by an individual or group of the social institutions of an ethnic group to which one does *not* belong. However, as in the case of acculturation, within an ethnically stratified society, the prime direction of assimilation tends to be towards penetration of the social institutions of the majority society, and the majority ethnic group. In this context, the concept assimilation, may be used to refer to the process of penetration, by members of various ethnic minorities, of the major social structural spheres (institutions) of the majority, in both public and private life. The degree of assimilation of a particular ethnic minority can be measured in terms of the proportionate representation of its members in the major public (economic, educational, legal and political) institutions of the majority *society* and in the private institutions and informal relationships of the majority *ethnic group*.

To reiterate briefly: in terms of ethnic group affiliation or membership, the concept assimilation may be used to refer to the process by which one becomes a recognized member of any (or all) of the social institutions of an ethnic group other than one's own. Within the context of majority-minority relations, it is the process whereby the minority ethnic member gains entrance into, that is, membership in, the social institutions of the majority society (public sphere) and the majority ethnic group (private sphere).

Assimilation of members of an ethnic minority into the majority society does not usually occur at the same rate or to the same degree in all structural (institutional) spheres of social life. Although patterns of assimilation vary from one ethnic minority to another, some spheres of social life are generally more open to ethnic minorities than are others, and thus tend to be penetrated first.

The process of assimilation (structural integration) may be divided for purposes of analysis into three major spheres:

1. *Secondary Assimilation*
Secondary assimilation refers to the entrance of mem-

bers of ethnic minorities into the formal, public sphere of secondary, economic, educational, legal and political institutions of the majority society.

2. *Primary Assimilation*

Primary assimilation refers to the entrance of members of ethnic minorities into the informal, private sphere of social clubs, cliques and primary social relationships of the majority ethnic group.

3. *Marital Assimilation or Amalgamation*

Marital assimilation or amalgamation refers to inter-ethnic marriage. Marital assimilation is the ultimate step in primary assimilation.

Secondary assimilation is far less difficult than is primary, and takes place much more rapidly. It is considerably easier for members of ethnic minorities to gain prestige through acquiring positions of power and privilege on the basis of their achievements in the public sphere, than to gain a commensurate degree of prestige in the private sphere of the majority ethnic group. For the latter is often based on *ascriptive* characteristics, and thus depends not on "what one does", but "who one is". Also, members of ethnic minorities are often unwilling to assimilate in the sphere of primary social relationships. Thus, assimilation in the public sphere usually precedes and often occurs in the absence of assimilation in the private sphere.

Assimilation in the private sphere of primary social relationships is predicated on the occurrence of two further types of integration: stereotypical integration and identificational integration.

STEREOTYPICAL INTEGRATION

Stereotypical integration refers to the degree of prejudice and discrimination in social relationships between members of different ethnic groupings. A high degree of stereotypical integration requires the minimization of social distance between the different ethnic categories resulting in a breakdown of the invisible wall and of social interaction in terms of ethnic stereotypes. It also implies the potentiality for acceptance and treatment of ethnic outsiders as insiders, that is, as social equals and as individual personalities. Viewed in the context of majority-minority relations the degree of stereotypical integration of ethnic minorities can be measured in terms of the extent to which social relationships between majority and minority ethnic categories are characterized by prejudice, discrimination and the employment of ethnic stereotypes.

IDENTIFICATIONAL INTEGRATION
Identificational integration refers to the process whereby an ethnic category or group to which one does not belong becomes one's *reference group*, that is, the category of people whose standards are used to evaluate and rank people. The degree of ethnic identificational integration can be measured in terms of the extent to which one's sense of self-identity is transferred from one's ethnic membership group to an ethnic category or group other than one's own. When full ethnic identificational integration takes place, any association or identification with one's original ethnic membership group has totally disappeared.

INTEGRATION AND ETHNICITY
Processes of acculturation and secondary assimilation of members of ethnic minorities into the public sphere of the majority society do not require a significant shift in ethnic identity or a change in ethnically-defined membership groups. Although acquisition of new reference groups and entrance into new membership groups is inevitable, these new referents and social institutions may be political, legal, economic, occupational or educational rather than *ethnic* in self-identificational focus and/or membership criteria. In other words, processes of integration in the public sphere of the majority society may involve, for members of ethnic minorities, a considerable expansion in their range of reference and membership groups. Thus one may acquire a variety of new (majority) reference and membership groups without necessarily abandoning old ones and without any significant dislocation in one's *ethnic* reference or membership group. In contrast, integration of ethnic minorities into the private

sphere of primary social relationships of the majority ethnic group is predicated on the occurrence of some degree of ethnic identificational integration. Assimilation in the private sphere requires that social distance between majority and minority ethnic members be minimized, that interaction no longer be predicated on ethnic stereotypes and that social relationships become individualized and personalized. In other words, primary assimilation is predicated on a relatively high degree of stereotypical integration. When this happens, the subjective indicators of ethnic group boundaries, separating ethnic outsider from insider lose salience, identification of minority ethnic (outsider) as majority ethnic (insider) is facilitated, and a major shift in ethnic reference group orientation (from minority to majority) may occur. When one's ethnic reference group orientation shifts radically, one may, at the same time, be an insider in terms of one's membership in a particular (minority) ethnic category, but an outsider in terms of one's primary (majority) reference group orientation. That is to say, one's primary ethnic reference group has changed, but one's ethnic membership group remains the same. The shift in ethnic reference group requires a shift in ethnic *self-definition*. For a change in ethnic *membership* group to occur, however, an alteration in both self and *other definitions* of ethnicity is required. One must both identify one's self and be identified by others (majority group members) as a member of the majority ethnic group.

Total integration into the majority ethnic group requires that minority ethnic members be accorded the status of insiders (full and equal members) by the majority ethnic group. This last stage in the process of integration—change in ethnic membership group—requires full primary assimilation. Primary assimilation is therefore the most important aspect of the assimilation process for ethnic minorities, for once it has occurred, the ultimate step, marital assimilation, will naturally follow.

Inter-ethnic marriage, within an ethnically-stratified society such as Canada, does not *necessarily* lead to total assimilation of the minority ethnic partner. Where the marriage is a source of continuing tension because of cultural and/or religious conflicts, the outcome, for one or both partners, may be one of *marginality*—a deep-seated feeling of ambivalence towards, or alienation from, both ethnic communities. On the other hand, the partners may seek a new synthesis, without total disavowal from either ethnic tradition.

TOTAL INTEGRATION OF AN ETHNIC MINORITY

Within the context of majority/minority ethnic relations, total integration requires that members of the ethnic minority will be willing to sever all ties with their original ethnic membership group and to shift both their loyalties and membership to the majority ethnic group. Even more importantly, in an ethnically stratified society, it requires that members of the majority ethnic group be willing to accept ethnic minority members as social equals and as individual personalities, and to allow them full participation in all majority social institutions in both public and private spheres. Complete integration has not taken place until the minority ethnic member is able to function as a full and equal member of the majority group in both the public and private spheres of social life.

When minority ethnic integration takes place fully in both cultural and structural terms, that is, total acculturation and assimilation, together with stereotypical and identificational integration, the minority ethnic group or category ceases to exist as a separate social entity. At the group level, total integration occurs with the large-scale shift in group membership from the minority to the majority ethnic group. When this happens, the minority ethnic grouping ceases to be a *viable* social category. Both its rationale for existence (self and other definitions of ethnicity) and its demographic basis for existence (actual and potential membership) have disappeared. With total integration the culture and social institutions of the minority ethnic group become extinct and the ethnic minority ceases to exist as a recognized social category. At the group level, total integration rarely occurs.

Our argument here has focussed on one-way acculturation and assimilation, from minority to majority—the
ideal-typical pattern of integration within ethnically
stratified societies such as Canada. This pattern of integration most closely approximates the "dominant conformity"
model (to be discussed more fully later). The reader
should remember, however, that all processes of integration are potentially two-way processes; hence the principles elucidated here may be empirically demonstrated in
a variety of patterns, ranging from a relatively comprehensive symmetric two-way exchange, leading towards a
"melting pot" outcome, to a highly asymmetric one-way
exchange favouring dominant conformity and leading to
total integration of the ethnic minority. Again, processes
of integration may be limited and controlled by either
or both minority and majority ethnic groups, favouring
cultural pluralism and leading towards the alleged "Canadian mosaic".

PROCESSES OF INTEGRATION AMONG CANADIAN INUIT GROUPS
    Acculturation (Cultural Integration). For almost a cen-
tury and a half (from about 1820 to 1960) contact between
Europeans and Euro-Canadians with Canada's remote
eastern high Arctic Inuit peoples was limited almost entirely to sporadic visits of fur traders, whalers, missionaries, and R.C.M.P. patrols. The acculturation process
between Inuit and European began with a limited and
relatively egalitarian cultural exchange of material and
technological items associated with the fur trade. Inuit
hunters and trappers exchanged skins, (bear, fox and
seal) and ivory (walrus tusks) for new, material items of
European technology such as rifles and boats. Until the
1950's, the demand for Euro-Canadian consumer goods
among the Inuit was small, and Hudson's Bay Fur Trading
posts carried little beyond supplies for hunting and trapping.
    Prior to a rapid and radical increase in the acculturation
process generated by the introduction of welfare and family allowances in the late 1940's, one of the most important
acculturative agents among the Inuit (as among the

Canadian Indians) was the missionary. From the early twentieth century, missionaries sought not only to convert the alleged "savages" to Christianity, but to fully resocialize them with a totally new world view and sense of morality based on the dominant values of Western, Judaeo-Christian culture (Ellis, 1971, p. 18). Non-literate Inuit peoples of the eastern high Arctic were taught to write in a new syllabic alphabet (originally designed by a Christian missionary for transcribing the Cree Indian language), for it was in the field of formal education that the greatest systematic effort towards acculturation of the Canadian Inuit was made. *Directed acculturation*—deliberate, conscious, systematic efforts to effect cultural change—was most successfully carried out within the insulated and protected "total environment" of the residential mission school. The language of instruction in mission schools was English (or French); thus, the entire educational process was predicated on linguistic acculturation. Moreover, mission schools not only taught the "three R's" and preached some version of Western, Christian morality but they also trained and rewarded children for achieving Euro-Canadian educational and occupational goals often totally unrelated to and incompatible with the Inuit hunting and trapping way of life. Within the residential school context, acculturation was by no means confined to the sphere of formal education. The daily encounter with new food items, for example, generated new Euro-Canadian tastes and wants. Thus, when similar food items began to appear in the Hudson's Bay stores, the demand, especially among the young, was more than equal to the supply. Most importantly, the mission school environment created a new need among the young for Euro-Canadian comforts: abundance of food and books, ample light and warmth, private space for study and sleeping, and a general standard of life far beyond the subsistence level. The acquisition of these new Euro-Canadian needs and wants made the traditional Inuit way of life appear (by way of contrast) increasingly difficult for the young.

Structural Integration: Economic Assimilation. Integration of the Canadian Inuit has, until recently, been largely confined to the sphere of cultural integration. No large-scale structural changes occurred until the end of World War II, when significant numbers of Inuit were hired as workers on construction of military air fields and other installations. The most portentous of these activities was construction of the D.E.W. line (distant early warning radar line), which was established across, what were, in the 1950's some of the most isolated Inuit regions in Arctic Canada (Hughes, 1965, p. 19). Probably the largest effect of the D.E.W. line was not so much the assimilation of substantial numbers of Inuit into the Euro-Canadian economic structure, but its powerful influence as a model of southern Euro-Canadian culture. Sudden exposure to a vast new range of opportunities, comforts and luxuries was overwhelming in its influence on Inuit peoples from remote settlements. Many Inuit, employed temporarily in wage work for the D.E.W. line became, in a short time, so imbued with Euro-Canadian wants and goals, that they no longer wanted to return to their traditional occupational pursuits in their home communities. When work opportunities in the new communities developed along the D.E.W. line sites were drastically reduced, many Inuit were, nevertheless, forced to return to their former homes. These more acculturated Inuit, strongly identifying with the Euro-Canadian reference group sought wage work in their home communities from the available Euro-Canadian agencies. Thus, a new structural division, based on degree of acculturation and economic assimilation developed between Inuit hunters and trappers on the one hand, and wage workers on the other. Penetration by the Inuit of Euro-Canadian economic institutions, though severely limited by the paucity of available wage work opportunities in the isolated settlements, nevertheless radically altered the traditional status system within Inuit communities.

Identificational Integration. Socio-economic divisions within Inuit communities today, reflect differences in degree of cultural and identificational integration among Inuit members (Vallee, 1917a). For those Inuit who aspire to Euro-Canadian ways, who prefer wage work to hunting and trapping, and who seek local agency jobs, the Euro-Canadian leaders (Hudson's Bay store manager, government agent, missionary, doctor, nurse, teacher, et al.) are looked to as models for behaviour and consulted in terms of decision-making. In other words, for the more acculturated Inuit, operating within the *parallel* work and status system, the primary reference group is Euro-Canadian. On the other hand, for the traditionally-oriented Inuit, preferring and living largely within the *alternate* hunting and trapping economy and status system, the great hunter is still the leader and authority figure par excellence and continues to provide the model to admire and emulate. For the less acculturated Inuit, the primary reference group remains Inuit.

Present-day Inuit settlements tend to be further segmented along generational lines, strongly linked to differences in degree of linguistic and educational integration. A growing number of young Inuit (c. 17-26 years of age) are essentially marginal in status and identification (Latowsky [Kallen] 1971-1972). This new category of marginal Inuit youth consists mainly of those Inuit who have lived for most of their formative years (c. 8-17 years of age), for nine months of the year, away from home, at residential mission schools. Most of these young people have completed their elementary education (c. grade 8) and are able to converse relatively fluently in English. Some have also acquired further "academic upgrading" in adult education courses, and/or pre-vocational training in special federal government programmes designed for indigenous peoples.

Largely through encouragement on the part of missionaries, teachers and government agents, these young Inuit have attempted to assimilate, educationally and occupationally, into Euro-Canadian society, only to find (in most cases) that they were insufficiently educated and trained for the available Euro-Canadian jobs. Moreover, many of these young people (particularly the more timid males) soon discovered that they lacked the requisite social skills for participation in the informal "after five" life of an urban, southern Euro-Canadian community such as Winnipeg, Montreal, Ottawa or Toronto; or even a "quasi-urban" northern community such as Fort Churchill or Frobisher Bay. At the same time, because of the long periods of time spent away from home in order to attain the required linguistic, educational and occupational skills for economic assimilation in the majority society, they had neglected learning the traditional skills which would make them productive members of the alternate (hunting and trapping) Inuit economy.

When these marginal youth return to their home communities, they are unable to integrate successfully within either the traditional (hunting and trapping) or the new (wage work) economic institutions within the settlement. Not only do they lack both the skills and the desire to participate effectively in hunting and trapping activities, but the menial type of wage work available from local Euro-Canadian agencies is usually incompatible with their newly acquired skills and interests and thus does not fulfil their occupational aspirations. Many of these young Inuit soon become bored and dissatisfied with their jobs and tend to leave or be fired after a short time. They shift from one job to another, and (sometimes) from one community to another unable to integrate successfully, more than temporarily or peripherally, within either Inuit or Euro-Canadian communities. While they tend to model themselves after Euro-Canadians and adopt a predominantly Euro-Canadian outlook and life style, their primary reference group seems to consist of their own peers; those Inuit youth having the same problems or still attending Euro-Canadian schools.

Although there has been a major shift in reference group orientation among these young Inuit, from minority to majority grouping, this has rarely led (as yet) to ethnic identificational integration. Most Inuit, even the most highly acculturated contemporary youth, do not consciously aspire to become *Kadluna* (pl. *at*) (the Inuit term for "White man" or Euro-Canadian). Their primary ethnic identity, strongly linked with the North and the Inuit people of the Canadian Arctic, remains Inuit.

Structural Integration. The major thrust of structural integration (assimilation) in contemporary Inuit communities is not towards increased participation, proficiency and social mobility of the Inuit population within the Euro-Canadian institutional framework, but rather towards increased *dependency* on Euro-Canadian social institutions (Ferguson, Honigmann, and Vallee, in Elliott, 1971). From the beginning, contemporary Inuit settlements were initiated and controlled by Euro-Canadian agents and agencies. Economic dependency on Euro-Canadian agencies has steadily increased as a result of the growth of the Inuit population and the rise in demand for Euro-Canadian consumer goods. Local, natural resources can no longer provide for the expanding needs and demands of the increasingly larger families of hunters and trappers. The Inuit, regardless of work preference, have thus become increasingly dependent on the limited and often temporary opportunities for wage work available at or through the Euro-Canadian agencies. But neither hunting and trapping, wage work, nor the combination of the two forms of economic activity, enable more than a few Inuit, at present, to be economically self-sufficient. Consequently, they have become more and more dependent on various kinds of government welfare assistance.

Economic dependency in the contemporary Inuit settlement is matched by political dependency. Although, today, there is increasing formal political representation and participation of the Inuit, structural integration of the Inuit in the political sphere of the majority society is only token. Most Inuit settlements have now attained local self-government, but Inuit settlement councils (the local organs of self-government) have not attained a position of economic or political strength from which to make demands from the territorial or federal governments. The status of their resolutions is merely that of recommendations which must be forwarded through several levels of local and regional bureaucratic government "red tape" before consideration in Yellowknife or Ottawa. Because they lack the power necessary to back their demands, the political position of the Inuit is one of a child asking for favours from a sometimes benevolent but often unbending parent.

In similar vein, at the national level, ultimate decision-making remains a Euro-Canadian prerogative. The Inuit Tapirisat (National Eskimo Brotherhood) is a socio-political organization funded by a federal government agency (the Department of the Secretary of State) and, therefore, dependent on the will of the Euro-Canadian majority for its continued existence. Although it purportedly represents the voice of the Canadian Inuit through their local, regional, and national leadership, its Inuit representatives lack the linguistic, educational, economic and political resources and skills *in Euro-Canadian terms,* necessary in order for them to be able to negotiate effectively with the more powerful Euro-Canadian government agencies, in their own (Inuit) interests.

Despite a massive post-war surge of contact between Inuit and Euro-Canadian, the secondary assimilation of Canadian Inuit into the educational, economic, legal and political institutions of Euro-Canadian society is minimal. The Inuit remain a "people under tutelage", increasingly dependent on Euro-Canadian government (agencies and agents) for their very survival.

Primary assimilation of the Inuit is blocked, in large part, by the overtly or covertly racist, segregationist policies of Euro-Canadian agencies and agents. In Frobisher Bay, for example, the Inuit have long been excluded from Euro-Canadian club rooms, including those operated under Canadian and American government auspices (Honigmann (comment) in Hughes, 1965, pp. 60-61). In most Inuit communities, social and residential segregation of Inuit from Euro-Canadian is clearly the norm (Ferguson, 1971, p. 25). Only very recently have some Inuit, especially the more highly educated and acculturated young people, come to recognize and resent the fact that they have been socially isolated from and discriminated against by the Euro-Canadian majority. In reaction, more and more Inuit are now beginning to more positively evaluate and to openly assert expressions of their distinctive Inuit culture, social institutions and identity (Vallee, 1971a, p. 126).

STEREOTYPICAL INTEGRATION AND MARITAL ASSIMILATION:
BARRIERS OF ETHNIC VISIBILITY

Stereotypical integration has proved to be extremely difficult not only for the Inuit, but for all of Canada's "visible" minorities: Indians, Inuit and Métis; Blacks, Chinese and Japanese. Among these ethnic minorities, skin colour and facial features serve as important social indicators of ethnicity, accounting for the minority's high visibility to outsiders, and (thus) facilitating the perpetuation of prejudicial attitudes and discriminatory practices on the part of the majority society. Discrimination against Blacks, Chinese and Japanese in Canada has been previously discussed in some detail. Similar attitudes and practices have historically prevailed towards Canadian Indians, Inuit, and Métis, but relative isolation of many of these groups of indigenous peoples has, until recently, restricted contact with Euro-Canadians and thus reduced the (reported) incidence of overt acts of discrimination. With the development of multi-ethnic Northern communities such as Inuvik, Fort Churchill, and Frobisher Bay, the reported incidence of discrimination against Indians, Inuit, and Métis (predicated on negative "racial" stereotypes) has greatly increased (Ferguson, Vranas and Stephens, and Honigmann in Elliott, 1971).

Marital assimilation of visible Canadian ethnic minorities has been largely blocked at the level of primary assimilation. Socially and residentially segregated from the dominant group, and subject to continuing discrimination on the basis of persistent, negative, ethnic stereotypes these minority ethnics are for the most part prevented from getting close enough to form intimate, personal relationships with majority members.

Historically, the outstanding Canadian example of large-scale inter-ethnic mating, in some cases leading to marriage between majority and "visible" minority members is provided in the case of the Métis. Métis is the Canadian name given people born from the union of Euro-Canadians (primarily French and Scottish fur traders and settlers) and indigenous peoples (primarily Indian women) (Valentine, 1971, p. 110). In the case of the Métis, inter-ethnic mating and marriage did not lead to marital assimilation into the dominant group, but rather, to the creation of a new, hybrid ethnic group, stigmatized as "half breeds" and continually discriminated against by both (indigenous) minority and (Euro-Canadian) majority groups (Slobodin, 1971).

PROCESSES OF ETHNIC INTEGRATION: SUMMARY

In much of the social scientific literature concerned with processes of ethnic integration, the concepts acculturation and assimilation have not been clearly differentiated, thus their usefulness as analytic tools has been somewhat impeded. In any study of inter-ethnic relations which focusses on the effects of continued contact on members of different ethnic categories, it is of the utmost importance to clearly delineate *what it is that is being affected* by the transactional processes occurring between different ethnic groups.

Acculturation or cultural integration (as here defined) is the process of ethnic integration whereby changes in a people's culture, reference group orientation and sense of identification occur. To the extent that the direction of cultural change is toward the norms, standards, values and patterns of the majority ethnic group, acculturation processes may be regarded as transactional processes whereby members of ethnic minorities acquire the cultural characteristics and skills of the majority, absorb the standards of the majority as norms for their own behaviour and identify with majority group members. Acculturation may be seen as a continuum from one polar extreme, in which a people's original culture remains intact, and there is no acquisition of distinctive, new (majority) cultural characteristics and skills (no acculturation), to the other polar extreme, in which a people's original culture disappears—through radical transformation or total absorption—and there is acquisition of and proficiency in using new (majority) characteristics and skills to a degree commensurate with majority group members.

The degree of acculturation of members of particular ethnic categories has important bearing on the question of their potential for assimilation. For it is through acculturation that members of ethnic minorities acquire the language, skills and qualifications required for penetration of (proportionate representation in) the major social institutions of the majority society. Acculturation is, moreover, the key to changes in reference group orientation and in self- and other-identity for members of ethnic minorities. Although a high degree of acculturation is not *necessarily* accompanied by changes in ethnic identity, acculturation paves the way for identificational integration by opening doors for minority ethnics to active participation in majority social institutions alongside members of the majority ethnic group(s).

Assimilation or structural integration (as here defined) is the process of ethnic integration whereby changes in a people's social institutions, membership groups and status or social position in society at large, take place. To the extent that structural change is directed towards penetration of major social institutions of the majority society, assimilation may be regarded as the process whereby members of ethnic minorities gain entrance into (become proportionately represented in) the political, legal, educational and economic institutions of the majority society in the public sphere, and in the clubs, cliques and primary social relationships of the majority ethnic group, in the private sphere. Assimilation implies changes in membership groups and status, and here, it is of crucial importance to distinguish between the public and private spheres of social life. In order for members of ethnic minorities to gain majority *ethnic* membership and status they must be accepted as majority members (insiders) in the private sphere of primary social relationships. Primary assimilation is, therefore, predicated on a high degree of stereotypical integration. Moreover, total assimilation, in *ethnic* terms, requires a total shift in both ethnic identification (full identificational integration) and in ethnic membership and status, from minority to majority ethnic group. Assimilation may be seen as a continuum from one polar extreme, in which a people's original social institutions remain intact and there is no penetration of majority social institutions (no assimilation) to the other polar extreme in which a people's original social institutions become extinct, and there is complete penetration of majority social institutions (total assimilation). Total ethnic integration in cultural, structural, stereotypical and identificational spheres rarely occurs at the group level. When this does happen, the original ethnic group or category becomes extinct.

FACTORS AFFECTING THE INTEGRATIONIST RESPONSES OF ETHNIC MINORITIES

The patterns of integration, as well as the rate and degree of acculturation and assimilation, may vary widely from one ethnic minority to another. Variations in integrationist responses of ethnic minorities are the result not only of differences in majority group(s) treatment of ethnic minorities, but also of differential orientations generated within minority ethnic communities. The invisible wall between majority and minority ethnic groups is predicated on ethnic group boundaries developed and maintained by *both* majority and minority communities. Thus the integrationist response of a given ethnic minority is a function of both internal (minority) and external (majority) variables affecting the degree of permeability of the invisible wall.

Several major variables may be utilized as social indicators or measures of ethnic integrationist tendencies:

1. *Degree of Physical, Cultural and Behavioural Similarities (or Disparities)*
   The greater the physical, cultural and behavioural dif-

ferences (actual or assumed) between minority and majority ethnic groupings the greater the barriers to minority ethnic integration.

2. Degree of Institutionalization of the Ethnic Hierarchy

The more highly institutionalized the ethnic hierarchy, that is, the more strongly legitimated through custom and/or law, the greater the barriers to integration of ethnic minorities.

*3. Degree of Social Distance**

The greater the degree of social distance between ethnic majority and minority, the greater the barriers to integration of ethnic minorities.

*4. Degree of Social Organization**

The greater the degree of social organization of the ethnic community (majority and/or minority) directed towards the goal of socio-cultural preservation the greater the barriers to minority ethnic integration.

*5. Degree of Social Integration**

The greater the degree of social integration or solidarity within the ethnic community (majority and/or minority) directed towards the goal of socio-cultural preservation the greater the barriers to minority ethnic integration.

6. Degree of Demographic Balance

The greater the ability of the ethnic group to maintain the requisite population numbers and sex ratio to guarantee recruitment of membership from within the ethnic grouping and to ensure socio-cultural preservation, the greater the barriers to minority ethnic integration.

7. Nature of the Contact Situation

The lesser the frequency and shorter the duration of contact, the more limited the spheres in which contact occurs, and the less direct (face-to-face) the social interaction between members of majority and minority ethnic groupings, the greater the barriers to minority ethnic integration.

8. Degree of Territorial Concentration (or Dispersion)

The greater the degree of territorial concentration of

*For fuller elaboration of these variables, see pp. 122-123.

the ethnic grouping (majority and/or minority) the greater the barriers to minority ethnic integration.

A comparative analysis of patterns of integration of Jews and Italians in Toronto, may serve to illustrate the foregoing principles. The reader should keep in mind the observation that a pattern or trend reported for any ethnic group will not necessarily apply in a different time period or in a different locality. Also, as has previously been pointed out, any observed pattern or trend of a given population may ignore incongruities in expressed behaviours of some members.

A COMPARISON OF INTEGRATIONIST RESPONSES OF JEWISH
AND ITALIAN MINORITIES IN PRESENT-DAY TORONTO
Degree of Similarities (Disparities). As European immigrants, both Jews and Italians in Toronto are generally quite similar to the Euro-Canadian majority in physical appearance. Differences in length of residence in Canada (duration of contact) and, (concomitantly) degree of acculturation, account in part for the present higher visibility of Italians. The largest wave of Italian immigration, from southern Italy, Sicily and Sardinia, has occurred since World War II; whereas Jewish immigration was heaviest at the turn of the twentieth century (1880 to 1920). Most of these Jewish immigrants came from Eastern Europe and many arrived with urban-orientated values and a complex of educational, occupational, and linguistic traditions and skills easily adaptable to the urban-Canadian context. Rapid and extensive acculturation of these Jewish immigrants was accompanied by a concomitant rise in socio-economic status and the achievement, by the second generation, of middle-class economic rank. By the time of the arrival of the largest wave of Italian immigration, most Torontonian Jews, despite their continued patterns of social clustering, had become virtually indistinguishable from their middle-class Euro-Canadian counterparts.

The more recent Italian immigrants are (presently) more highly visible than the Jews in Toronto, due to their retention of traditional modes of dress and demeanour and in their continuing to speak in the Italian language. The large numbers of "sponsored" Italian immigrants, coming from the depressed rural areas of southern Italy and Sicily, lack not only the requisite linguistic skills, but also the appropriate occupational, educational and social skills which would facilitate their integration into the highly industrialized, urban environment of Toronto. Consequently, many new Italian immigrants tend, at least initially, to remain within easy reach of their "sponsors" (family and relatives), upon whom they depend for emotional and financial support, and who serve as interpreters of/and contact agents with the new, Canadian society. Occupational as well as residential clustering of Italian immigrants contributes to their present high visibility. Employment agencies favour placement of Italian immigrants with fellow Italians who speak the same language. The resultant concentration of Italians in particular areas of manual labour, such as construction, reinforces the prevailing stereotype of the unskilled Italian construction worker, and contributes to the present high level of immigrant Italian visibility.

Degree of Social Distance. In Toronto, ethnic group boundaries appear to be stronger and more clearly defined among Jews than among Italians. Probably the major factor behind the clarity and strength of ethnic group boundaries among Jews is the fact that the Jewish ethnic and cultural heritage has, historically, been inextricably interwoven with a continuing, strong religious tradition. Judaic tradition (religious and customary) is rooted in the ethnocentric premise of the "Chosen People": the belief that Jews, through obedience to Judaic law (613 commandments) are destined to become a "source of light unto the nations"; that is, to provide the exemplary way of life for all nations of mankind to follow (Werblowsky and Wigoder, 1965, pp. 87-88). Although contemporary Torontonian Jews (except the committed Orthodox) no longer accept the "Chosen People" concept in its literal form, many tend, nevertheless, to assume that the Jewish way of life—the historical and cultural heritage of their ancestors—is in many ways morally and ethically superior to that of non-Jews. This continuing high degree of ethnocentrism encourages the persistence, in practice, of the religious prohibition against intermarriage, despite a sharp decline in religiosity. Fear of intermarriage, in turn, serves to prohibit or discourage intimate social contacts beyond the ethnic group. Also, customary observance of the religious tenet of collective responsibility—of each Jew for every Jew—encourages a continuing high degree of active participation in a wide variety of ethnic institutions, religious and secular, and thus facilitates a high degree of primary interaction within the ethnic group. A long history of persecution as a religious and ethnic minority combined with a traditionally high degree of ethnocentrism operates to keep the level of social distance between Jewish insiders and non-Jewish outsiders relatively high. As a result, even some of the most acculturated Jews tend to voluntarily limit social relationships with non-Jews to the impersonal, public sphere of secondary, majority institutions, and to associate on a close, personal level largely or entirely with fellow Jews (Latowsky [Kallen], 1971, pp.107-109).

Although Italians in Toronto share a common religion (Catholicism) the religious tradition is not, as in the case of the Jews, inextricably interwoven with a continuing strong cultural heritage and sense of ethnic identity. The Catholic religious community is not ethnically exclusive, as is the Jewish, and consequently Catholic parishes in Toronto are not exclusively Italian in membership. Moreover, Catholicism, within the Toronto Italian community does not appear to function as a strong integrating force within the community. Thus the religious prohibition against intermarriage with non-Catholics does not act simultaneously among Italians, as in the case of the Jews, to strengthen ethnic group boundaries. Accordingly, the rate of intermarriage between Italians and non-Italians in Toronto increases considerably more with duration of contact and degree of acculturation than does the rate of intermarriage between Jews and non-Jews (Latowsky [Kallen], p. 100, Ziegler, p. 119).

In contrast to Jews, whose religiously-defined sense of

collective (ethnic) responsibility extends to all Jews, everywhere, the Italian sense of collective responsibility appears to be limited to a small family-based circle of kin and friends. Several American authors (Gans, 1962, Glazer and Moynihan, 1963) have suggested that feelings of distrust and hostility towards outsiders among Italian-Americans are rooted in a tradition of "amoral familism", that is, categorical, utilitarian and potentially exploitive social relationships with outsiders (everyone outside of the recognized family clique). This tradition appears to have developed as a survival technique among poverty-stricken peasants in the rural villages of southern Italy (Banfield, 1958). As expressed among contemporary Italian-Americans, the degree of distrust of particular categories of outsiders is related to the degree of disparities between insiders (family-based circle of relatives and friends) and all others. Thus distrust of non-Italians and non-Catholics is higher than distrust of Italian Catholics. Although the degree of ethnocentrism among Italians as an ethnic category is low, the degree of social distance between Italians and non-Italians is considerably higher than is the degree of social distance between fellow-Italians.

Given the fact that the heaviest wave of (recent) Italian immigration to Toronto has been from the rural villages of southern Italy, Sicily and Sardinia, one might suppose that expressions of distrust of outsiders among Italian immigrants to Canada would not be too different from those found among Italian-Americans. This hypothesis is supported by the findings of Ziegler (1972, pp. 66, 71-73), which clearly indicate that Italians in Toronto conform to a high degree to the American pattern. Like their American counterparts, they tend to focus their private social lives around a close-knit family circle of relatives and friends. Moreover, expressions of prejudice and hostility against outsiders are, as in the United States, related to the degree of perceived disparities between insiders and outsiders (Ziegler, pp. 79-81). Accordingly, newer Italian immigrants tend to limit their intimate social relationships largely to fellow-Italians; whereas the more acculturated,

native-born Italians interact more freely and frequently
with outsiders and may even include non-Italians within
their private, family-based social world.

Territorial Concentration and Demographic Balance.
Both the Jewish and Italian ethnic communities in
Toronto with populations of 101,415 and 250,190 respectively (1971 census), have the requisite numerical strength
and sex-ratio balance to enable them to persist as distinct
ethnic groups through recruitment of membership from
within the minority ethnic category. Moreover, the Italian
and Jewish communities are the most highly residentially-
concentrated of all minority ethnic groups in Toronto
(Richmond, 1972).

In the case of the Italian ethnic minority, the present
pattern of residential concentration among the immigrant
generation is due, in large part, to the fact that most of
the recent post-war Italian immigration has been sponsored or nominated (Richmond, 1972, p. 50). New immigrants tend to live with or close to relatives and friends
who have helped them come to Toronto and who are
responsible, at least initially, for their economic and
socio-psychological welfare. In addition, the effect of
"chain migration" is that Italians from the same village
of origin in Italy tend to cluster in the same area; thus the
tendency towards residential concentration among Italians
in Toronto has been strongly reinforced through post-war
immigration patterns.

In the case of Jews, voluntary residential concentration
has, historically, been predicated on religious rules and
customary practices requiring continuous, first-hand contact among community members. In Eastern Europe, the
pattern of voluntary concentration was continually reinforced through discrimination against Jews, and, periodi-
cally, social and residential segregation of the Jewish
minority was legally enforced through government edict.
In Canada, as in Europe, residential concentration and
segregation of Jewish communities has been in part
voluntary and in part a reaction to continuing forces of
prejudice and discrimination against the Jewish minority.

Prior to the enactment and enforcement of anti-discriminatory laws in the 1940's, discrimination against Jews in Ontario, in the area of housing, strongly reinforced the historical tendency towards clustering of the Jewish group in residential ethnic enclaves. Today, despite the reduction of overt discrimination against Jews and the achievement of middle-class socio-economic status, affording most Jews increased opportunities for residential dispersion, the Jewish ethnic minority remains, voluntarily, residentially highly concentrated in Toronto.

In both the Jewish and (immigrant) Italian communities, the continuing high level of residential concentration serves to facilitate and expand opportunities for informal, social contacts with insiders. As an indirect result, social relationships with outsiders tend to be limited to the formal, public sphere of majority institutions, and primary assimilation is impeded, in part, from within the minority ethnic group itself. However, when duration of contact is taken into account, significant differences between the two communities become apparent. Within the Italian community, upward socio-economic mobility and increased acculturation are accompanied by residential dispersion and a marked increase in ethnic intermarriage (Ziegler, p. 119). With increased duration of contact, the Italian community has become increasingly segmented along socio-economic class lines with significant disparities between the close-knit immigrant sector and the more assimilationist-oriented middle-class category. In contrast, and numerous observed exceptions notwithstanding, a relatively large proportion of Jews remain residentially highly concentrated despite extensive acculturation and secondary assimilation. The degree of residential concentration among Jews corresponds roughly with the degree of religious acculturation as measured by membership in more traditional (Orthodox and Conservative) vis-à-vis more liberal (Reform) synagogue congregations (Richmond, 1972, p. 48). Despite these internal differences, however, the Jewish ethnic category remains the most highly residentially-concentrated of all the religiously-defined ethnic minorities in Toronto (*Ibid.* p. 41) and strong, negative attitudes toward intermarriage prevail even among most highly-acculturated, Reform Jews (Latowsky [Kallen], 1971, pp. 107-109).

The rates of Jewish endogamy reported in Book IV of the Royal Commission on Bilingualism and Biculturalism (page 291) are the highest of all ethnic groups in Canada: Jewish males, 1951—93.1 per cent; 1961—91.1 per cent; Jewish females, 1951—95.6 per cent; 1961—93.0 per cent. More recent figures are in the category of informed guesses; they place the current rate of overall Jewish-non-Jewish intermarriage at 15 per cent to 18 per cent in Canada. In effect, the Jewish community is still highly endogamous, but is far from being an island. All characteristics of the Jewish population in Canada are subject to one general trend: they are becoming more and more like those of other people they are living with. As in Canada, the figures for intermarriage in the U.S.A. show marked regional disparities. They indicate a clear, positive correlation between degree of Jewish residential concentration and degree of endogamy. For example, only 4.4 per cent of Jewish marriages reported for Springfield, Massachusetts (1966) were exogamous, whereas a figure of 48.8 per cent of exogamous Jewish marriages was reported for the state of Indiana, 1960-1963 (Sklare, 1971). A report based on the *National Jewish Population Study* (New York, The Council of Jewish Federations and Welfare Funds, 1973) suggests that the current proportion of intermarried Jewish persons is much higher than for previous periods; it gives a national figure of 31.7 per cent exogamous marriages in the U.S.A. between 1966 and 1972. Once more, this figure which shows that almost one-third of Jewish persons now marrying in the U.S.A. are intermarrying obscures regional disparities.

In Canada, the highest rates of Jewish endogamy are reported for Quebec, Ontario and Manitoba (Book IV, Royal Commission on Bilingualism and Biculturalism, pp. 294-295). These areas contain the most highly concentrated pockets of Jewish population—in Montreal,

Toronto, and Winnipeg, respectively. In the light of the U.S.A. material we may infer that in these urban areas—and Toronto in particular—the rates of Jewish endogamy are highest. (See also Rosenberg, 1971, Vol. 2, Ch. 5, pp. 84-87.) With respect to degree of endogamy, as such, Canadian conditions and rates do not seem to parallel those in the U.S.A.; similarly, there is reason to believe that Quebec-Ontario circumstances differ markedly from each other, partly due to a large influx to Quebec in recent years of French-speaking North-African Jews.

Degree of Social Organization. Both Jewish and Italian communities in Toronto tend to be highly institutionally complete. Residential ethnic enclaves are replete with a multitude of ethnically distinctive restaurants, stores, newspapers, and social, recreational and cultural organizations.

Striking differences, are, however, apparent in the area of employment. In the case of Jews, attainment of higher education and professional occupation has been accompanied by increased diversity and dispersion in the work situation. Italian immigrants tend, on the other hand, to be ethnically concentrated in the work situation. The majority of Italian immigrants are labourers and have jobs where co-workers are largely Italian (Jansen, 1971, p. 212). Although both communities afford members considerable opportunities for social interaction in the sphere of voluntary ethnic organizations, there appear to be significant differences between the two communities in the degree of actual membership and active participation of membership in these minority ethnic institutions. Also, the Jewish and Italian communities appear to differ in the extent to which social interaction within the various ethnic organizations generates and sustains a broader sense of ethnic community consciousness. In contrast to the Jewish people, Italians have no historical, ethnic or religious tradition of collective responsibility, upon which to build community-wide institutions geared to ethnic-group preservation. Italian sense of collective responsibility continues, as traditionally, to be limited largely to the family circle, and ethnic identity among Italians in Toronto rarely extends beyond the traditional, local or regional Italian community level. Accordingly, Italians tend to belong to few voluntary ethnic organizations and those they do belong to, tend to have a kinship, local or regional-Italian basis. This persistence of traditional Italian factional interests within the Toronto Italian community prevents co-operation between members of the various ethnic institutions at the community level, and impedes the development of a common sense of ethnic community consciousness in Toronto. As a result, community-wide organizations purportedly representing the entire Italian Toronto community (to outsiders) are in fact arbitrary confederations of loosely-linked and often socially distant, regional, local, religious, class or kin-based ethnic institutions representing diverse factional interests. This lack of social integration within the Italian community impedes the ability of ethnic leaders to overcome personal and factional differences between themselves and to corral support from their respective constituencies for community-wide projects. Thus, despite a high degree of institutional completeness, internal, institutional fragmentation of the Italian community impedes the ability of leadership and membership to unite and co-operate in order to take concerted action in the interests of the ethnic category as a whole (Jansen, 1969, 1971).

In contrast to Italians, Jews in Toronto tend to belong to and actively participate in a wide variety of voluntary ethnic and religious organizations. Because the traditional Judaic tenet of collective responsibility is customarily associated with participation in Jewish socio-cultural, educational, religious and philanthropic institutions, factional interests between the various ethnic and religious organizations do not prevent close co-operation of leadership and membership in community-wide projects. Both ethnic leadership and membership tend to feel a religious and/or customary obligation to overcome personal and factional interests in order to take concerted action in the interests of the ethnic community as a whole. The con-

tinuing success of community-wide philanthrophic en-
deavours such as the annual U.J.A. (United Jewish
Appeal) and Israel Bond Drives, as well as special campaigns in aid of fellow-Jews illustrate this principle.
Emergency campaigns in aid of Soviet Jews, as well as felt
crises such as the Yom Kippur War (October, 1973),
depend upon the ability of leadership to corral the support and co-operation of the community as a whole,
through the *combined efforts* of various institutions. Thus,
a continuing high level of active participation by Torontonian Jews in a variety of minority ethnic institutions
serves to generate a sense of "Toronto Jewish community"
consciousness, as well as to reinforce a broader sense of
ethnic identity with all Jews.

Degree of Social Integration. Despite internal segmentation of the Toronto Jewish community along lines of
country of origin, period of immigration, religious denom-
inational affiliation or non-affiliation, and degree of acculturation, the persistence of a high positive level of ethnic
identity among members facilitates community-wide co-
operation in the interests of the ethnic group as a whole.
Traditionally, "Jewishness" (Jewish ethnic identity), was
clearly, positively associated with "Judaism" (Judaic
religious identity). In contemporary Toronto, however,
this traditional linkage between religiosity and ethnicity
is strongly apparent only among the small minority of
committed (practising) Orthodox Jews. Most Jewish
Torontonians are not religious, either in terms of self-
definition or in terms of their acceptance of religious
tenets and/or observance of ritual practices. Few attend
synagogue services more than once a year (on High Holy
days). For many religiously-affiliated Jews, especially
members of Conservative and Reform congregations, the
most important function of the contemporary synagogue
seems to be that of education. Parents' emphasis on religious indoctrination of their children, has the primary
purpose of ensuring the persistance of Jewish ethnic
identity and commitment among the younger generation.
Today, both within and outside of the religious institu-

tional context, Jewish identity is increasingly focussed on the state of Israel: educational, cultural and philanthropic activities stress the learning of the Hebrew language as spoken in Israel; the importance of Israeli history and culture; promotion of all kinds of "package tours" to Israel; and continued financial support of all facets of Israeli growth and development. For the increasing numbers of professedly non-religious Jews—especially the youth— Israeli nationhood appears to be providing a viable alternative to Judaism as a primary focus for Jewish ethnic identity and vehicle for ethnic group preservation (Latowsky [Kallen], 109-110).

Unlike Jews, the Italian population in Toronto has neither a national nor a religious tradition of "Italian" ethnic identity. First-generation Italian immigrants continue, as in their homeland, to identify—beyond the family circle—mainly on a local level, with fellow Italians from the same hometown or village. In addition, the historical, regional rift between northern and southern Italians persists to some degree in Toronto. Given the (previously discussed) high degree of internal factionalism and institutional fragmentation within the Toronto Italian community, it is not surprising that Italian ethnic identity has been found to decrease sharply with length of residence or duration of contact (Ziegler, pp. 115-116).

The comparative analysis of the internal structures of the contemporary Jewish and Italian communities in Toronto, seems to indicate that ethnic group boundaries are far stronger and less permeable among Jews than Italians, and, concomitantly, suggests that the rate and degree of integration of Italians, vis-à-vis Jews is likely to increase to a far greater extent with length of residence (duration of contact). However, the rate and degree of integration of any ethnic minority is dependent not only on the relative strength of preservationist versus integrationist tendencies generated within the minority ethnic community, but also on the willingness or unwillingness of the majority to allow large-scale penetration of its social institutions by members of the particular ethnic minority.

Given these considerations, factors which are likely to retard or impede integration of Jews and/or Italians into the majority Euro-Canadian society *from without*, must (here) be taken into account.

Degree of Prejudice and Discrimination by Majority Group Members. From the turn of the century to the late 1940's, Jews in Ontario, were excluded from a wide variety of majority social institutions, including social and recreational organizations, professional schools and university courses, occupations, residential areas, beaches, parks and hotels. Today, although there is some evidence of continuing discrimination against Jews in the areas of employment, enrolment in university courses and entrance into private clubs, the level of overt discrimination, especially in the public sphere, has decreased significantly (Richmond, 1967, pp. 78-84). Because of their long, historical experience of oppression as a religious and ethnic minority, Jews have become highly sensitive to all forms of *anti-semitism*, overt and covert. As a result, a high level of consciousness of prejudice and discrimination is maintained among Jews. This serves to perpetuate barriers of social distance between Jewish insider and non-Jewish outsider, even when overt manifestations of anti-semitism are rare.

In contrast to the experience of early Eastern European Jewish immigrants who were constantly faced with overt acts of discrimination by majority group members, recent Italian immigrants to Toronto have been subjected far less to differential treatment. Nevertheless, covert forms of discrimination, especially against new Italian immigrants, persist. The male Italian immigrant continues to be viewed and treated by dominant group members in terms of persistent Italian ethnic stereotypes which depict him as an unskilled manual labourer. Thus, Italian newcomers are "expected" to fill menial labour and construction jobs. Not only has Canadian immigration policy (prior to 1967) encouraged Italians to come to Canada mainly to fill semi- and unskilled jobs, but Canadian employers have often been unwilling to hire qualified Italians for skilled occupations (Jansen, 1971, p. 212).

Prejudice and discrimination against Jews and Italians in Toronto continues to retard, but not to prevent, large-scale assimilation of members of these ethnic minorities in the public sphere of the majority society. For those Jews and Italians who have acquired the requisite skills, achievement of high-ranking (elite) positions in the economic and political spheres of the majority society is rapidly increasing. Today, it is in the private sphere of informal clubs, cliques and primary social relationships of the majority ethnic group, that a high level of prejudice and discrimination, and a continuing high level of social distance on the part of majority members, continues to operate to exclude all but a token few Jews and Italians (Kelner, 1971). *Degree of Institutionalization of the Ethnic Stratification System.* The Canadian ethnic hierarchy has little sanction in custom or law as applied to European immigrant ethnic groups such as Jews and Italians. Moreover, with the enactment of anti-discrimination legislation and enforcement in almost all provinces of human rights codes, opportunities for upward social mobility have greatly increased, for Italians and Jews alike. Customary practice, in Toronto as elsewhere, lags behind legal change, but for Italians and Jews rapidly acquiring the requisite skills, penetration of majority social institutions in the public sphere is becoming far less difficult than was (historically) the case. The present climate of ethnic protest on the part of many Canadian minorities and Prime Minister Trudeau's multicultural response (1970) indicates that the established Canadian system of ethnic stratification is now under serious question. Under present conditions, the stratification system cannot be said to be rigidly institutionalized and the rate and the degree of secondary structural integration of both Italian and Jewish ethnic minorities is likely to increase. *Degree of Internal Organization of Majority Community.* The degree of organization of the Euro-Canadian majority against assimilation of ethnic minorities such as Jews and Italians, increases as one ascends the ethnic hierarchy. Torontonian Jews have already made substantial gains in penetrating the political, legal, educational and economic institutions of the majority society, and Italians are rapidly following suit. Nevertheless, the apex of the majority society, in both the public and private spheres of ultimate decision-making, remains a tightly organized British-Canadian preserve. Interlocking directorships of major corporations present a solid, united front against assimilation of minority ethnics in the public sphere. In addition, membership in the ethnically exclusive, private social clubs and cliques of the majority social elite, reinforces on an informal level, the more formal bonds forged in the public sphere of interaction. In this way, at the apex of the majority elite, a continuing high degree of organization in both public and private spheres operates to prevent primary assimilation of members of both the Italian and Jewish ethnic minorities (Kelner, 1971).

Summary. A comparison of the patterns of integration of the Jewish and Italian ethnic minorities in Toronto indicates that the major forces operating within both majority and minority ethnic communities to prevent or impede integration occur in the area of primary assimilation. Not only is the majority society more highly organized in terms of preventing integration of ethnic minorities such as Jews and Italians in the private sphere of primary social relationships, but many members of both Jewish and Italian minorities prefer, at present, to limit their own primary social relationships to ethnic insiders.

Both Jewish and Italian communities in Toronto are residentially highly concentrated and highly complete institutionally, thus offering and facilitating opportunities for close, everyday contact with ethnic insiders. The Jewish community tends, however, to be far more strongly and positively ethnically identified and more highly organized and integrated for purposes of ethnic group preservation, than does the Italian. Thus, centripetal forces, such as religious and/or customary prohibitions against intermarriage, continue to keep most members of the Jewish ethnic community within the fold. Within the Italian ethnic minority, on the other hand, centrifugal (assimilationist) forces appear (over time) to be stronger than ethnic bonds. Internal factionalism and institutional fragmentation within the Italian community inhibit the development of a strong, collective community consciousness. Increased duration of contact is thus accompanied by a decrease in ethnic identity, an increase in residential dispersion and an increase in the rate of intermarriage. On the basis of the present evidence, it seems likely that future generations of Italian-Canadians in Toronto will make a more concerted effort than will Jewish-Canadians to penetrate the private sphere of the majority society, and, given the willingness of the majority, to assimilate at the primary level into the majority ethnic group.

MODELS OF ETHNIC INTEGRATION

In Canada, as in the United States, three models of ethnic integration have, for a long time, dominated social scientific discussion of majority/minority relations: Anglo-conformity, Melting pot and Cultural pluralism or Multi-culturalism. Each of these models contains somewhat different assumptions about the nature of ethnic integration processes, and about the kind of society which is predicated upon them or results from them. It is important to remember that these models are "ideal types" which do not exactly correspond with the empirical picture of minority ethnic integration within any society, at any given time. Nor do they exhaust the range of conceptual possibilities. For example, the model of a plural society in which different ethnic groups co-exist symbiotically, in a permanent state of peripheral contact, has never received serious attention from Canadian or American scholars writing about their own countries. It is also important to note that the model emphasized by majority group policies at one period, in a given society or societal region, may be discarded, under changing social conditions, for another. Most importantly, in a multi-ethnic society, the model adopted by the majority, as well as the response of the minority, may vary with the particular ethnic groups or categories in contact.

Anglo-Conformity (Dominant or Majority Group Con-

formity). The Anglo-conformity model (and its French-Canadian counterpart, Franco-conformity) requires the renunciation of the ethnic minority's ancestral culture in favour of the values, standards and life styles of the majority ethnic group. Because the model was originally conceived within a society in which the dominant ethnic group was generally categorized as "Anglo-Saxon", the particularized concept Anglo-conformity was employed to refer to the broader notion of dominant or majority group conformity.

Dominant group conformity assumes a one-way process of required acculturation. This model assumes a considerable status (power, privilege and prestige) differential between ethnic groups coming into contact, which enables one group to require the other to acculturate. Given these disparities, continuous contact between the ethnic groups results in the development of majority/minority relationships favouring the persistence and dominance of the culture and social institutions of the majority ethnic group, and the subordination or extinction of the ancestral culture and social institutions of the ethnic minority.

The Anglo-conformity model does not contain assumptions about assimilation: it does not specify whether or not the majority ethnic group will facilitate or impede penetration of its major social institutions by minority ethnics. However, since acculturation is *required,* there is an assumption of a high degree of ethnocentrism among majority members, and it follows that the willingness of the majority to allow assimilation will be affected by the relative degree of physical, cultural and behavioural similarities (or disparities) between the majority and the particular minority ethnic group(s) in contact. Thus minority ethnic integration will most likely be predicated on both achieved and ascribed criteria. Since some (unspecified) degree of acculturation is required for all ethnic minorities, the model assumes some social interaction between ethnic groups resulting in some sharing of values, goals, and behaviours, the acquisition of new (majority) reference groups and the possibility of developing a common sense of national identity. Whether or not a specific minority ethnic culture will become extinct because of total acculturation and whether or not a specific minority ethnic group will be totally absorbed by the majority (total integration) are questions which remain unresolved.

Melting Pot. The melting pot model requires a two-way process of both acculturation and assimilation between the ethnic groups in contact. This model assumes extensive social interaction in both public and private spheres between two (or more) ethnic groups, each relatively equal in terms of power, privilege, and prestige, and each exhibiting a relatively low degree of ethnocentrism. In the transactional processes of contact between the groups, each contributes equally to a merging and blending of peoples, cultures and social institutions. Given these prerequisites, continuous first-hand contact between the ethnic groups results in a radical transformation of the characteristics of both groups and the eventual development of one distinctive, new culture, society and ethnic unit. The melting pot model leaves no room for the overt persistence of the ancestral culture, social institutions or ethnic identity of either (any) group in contact. This model assumes that in the new society so created, social institutions will be easy to penetrate because there will be no ascriptive barriers to ethnic integration. Since the society is predicated on mutual social and cultural exchange and sharing, it also encourages and facilitates the development of a common sense of national/*ethnic* identity or peoplehood.

Cultural Pluralism (Multi-culturalism or Mosaic). The cultural pluralism model requires that processes of acculturation and assimilation be limited and controlled. Cultural pluralism requires some (unspecified) degree of integration (acculturation and assimilation) on the part of constituent groupings, necessary for effective participation (proportionate representation) of their members within the public sphere of secondary, societal institutions. At the same time the cultural pluralism model requires some (unspecified) degree of social segregation on the part of ethnic groupings, necessary for the maintenance and growth of the distinctive (ancestral) culture, identity and integrity of the various ethnic groups. This requirement assumes both a relatively high level of ethnocentrism and some degree of structural pluralism—development and maintenance of exclusive, primary social institutions —in the private sphere of the constituent ethnic units. Further, the cultural pluralism model assumes relative equality (in terms of power, privilege, and prestige) *and* ascriptive barriers to integration, between the ethnic groups in contact. In effect, it assumes an invisible wall because of which social interaction is limited and controlled. However, the degree of integration/segregation encouraged or allowed is not specified in this model. Cultural pluralism thus permits a wide range of variation in the degree of acculturation and assimilation (on the one hand) and the degree of persistence of the ancestral culture, social institutions and ethnic identity (on the other). A society predicated on cultural pluralism could, at the same time, encourage a common sense of national identity and a distinctive sense of ancestral or ethnic identity. The cultural pluralism model encourages the development of a hyphenated (national-ethnic, ethnic-national) identity.

The melting pot model has been widely heralded as the American ideal, in contrast to the ideal of cultural pluralism promulgated in Canada. This difference in current, national ideologies is reflected in the terms of reference typically employed by national leaders in addressing their citizens and would-be citizens. For example, President Ford addresses "the American people" or "fellow Americans", whereas Prime Minister Trudeau speaks to (or of) "all of Canada's peoples and cultures". Nevertheless, in neither the Canadian nor the American case, has the ideal model, at any time, clearly corresponded with the empirical picture of ethnic integration in society at large. It is probably true, that the United States has, over time exhibited more "melting pot" tendencies than has Canada. Conversely, Canada presently more closely resembles the multi-culturalism model than her American neighbour

does. The predominant pattern, however, in both countries, has historically been one of dominant conformity.

The Canadian Case. Following Confederation, the official Canadian ideology was one of cultural *dualism,* giving
recognition to the coexistence of distinctive English- and
French-Canadian cultures and social institutions. However, investigations undertaken by the Royal Commission
on Bilingualism and Biculturalism in the 1960's, provide
substantial evidence to support the current French-
Canadian claim that the predominant Canadian model
of integration has generally been one of Anglo-conformity.

Writings of English Canadians in the early twentieth
century, indicate that the prevailing ideology was, at
this time, one of Anglo-conformity (Woodsworth, 1972).
The English Canadians' sense of Canadian nationalism
linked pride in their new country with continuing pride
in their alleged "Anglo-Saxon" ethnic heritage, both of
which were strongly associated with ties and loyalties to
the British Crown. Thus many English Canadians were,
from the beginning, supportive of the view that Canada
should develop as a British preserve and an Anglo-Saxon
nation. Racial extremists of the day argued that since
people of a purported "inferior racial type" could not be
assimilated to the Anglo-Saxon model (because of their
racially-defined distinctiveness) they should be barred
from immigration to Canada. To admit them (the racists
argued) posed the threat of miscegenation and its alleged
inevitable consequences—the eventual corruption of the
"pure" Anglo-Saxon stock; the (concomitant) destruction
of the "higher (Anglo-Saxon) civilization"; and the decay
and ruination of the new Canadian nation. Most English
Canadians, however, were more optimistic about immigration, assuming that the dominant, so-called "Anglo-Saxon
race" with its supposed superior initiative and strength
could acculturate all newcomers to its "higher" ideals and
standards. This assumption was less overtly racist than
that of the extremists, in that it implied the cultural
(rather than the biological) superiority of the Anglo-Saxon
group and thus allowed the possibility of acculturation of

newcomers in the direction of Anglo-Saxon norms. The basic premise of this dominant view and the immigration policy predicated upon it, was that immigrants were welcome only if they could and would conform to the standards of the majority culture. The cultural standards, to which conformity of all newcomers was required, were based on what were assumed to be distinctive and superior Anglo-Saxon, Protestant values, and the ideal model was clearly White, Anglo-Saxon, Protestant (WASP).

Despite perceived cultural and religious differences, non-Anglo-Saxon, Protestant immigration was not believed to pose a real danger to the nation as long as it was assumed that the "superior" Anglo-Saxons would dominate, and that the new immigrants could be acculturated to the ways of the majority through the concerted efforts of members of the dominant group (especially educators and missionaries). Not all ethnic groups were, however, believed to be capable of acculturating to the Anglo-Saxon ideal. Distinctions were clearly drawn between the supposedly "lower" ethnic groups (for example, peoples from southern and eastern Europe) who were believed to be capable of acculturation, and the alleged "inferior races", marked and isolated by a skin colour barrier, who were assumed to be incapable of so doing. This racist ideology —one version of the "White supremacy" theory—was utilized to justify exclusion of many peoples, racially-defined as "Blacks" or "Negroes" and "Orientals". These alleged "ineducable" ethnic groups, it was believed, should be rigorously prevented from immigrating to Canada (Woodsworth, 1972, pp. X-XXII).

Over the years, with changing social conditions and subsequent changes in immigration policies, Canada has become increasingly multi-ethnic in population composition. As an indirect result, the early twentieth century model of Anglo-conformity, with its clearly racist bias, no longer has the overt sanction and support of public opinion. Among Canada's non-British and non-French populations—a category now constituting almost one third of Canada's peoples—the climate of opinion is clearly swinging away from passive acceptance of dominant conformity in favour of active encouragement of cultural pluralism. Spearheaded by Ukrainian spokesmen, the demands of the "other ethnic groups" (allegedly a potential "Third Force" in the Canadian political arena) gave rise, in 1969, to Book IV of the *Report of the Royal Commission on Bilingualism and Biculturalism*: "The Cultural Contribution of the Other Ethnic Groups". This document contains sixteen recommendations for the implementation of an official government policy of multi-lingualism and multi-culturalism.

Prime Minister Trudeau's announcement of a multi-cultural policy for Canada, on October 8, 1971, was the official response of the federal government to the recommendations contained in Book IV. On this occasion, Mr. Trudeau made it clear that although the government endorsed the "spirit" of Book IV, it did not support the position, implicit in its recommendations, that language and culture are indivisible. The federal government has rejected the notion that multi-culturalism necessitates multi-lingualism and has proposed that the multi-cultural policy be implemented within a bilingual framework.

The Prime Minister emphasized the fact, that under the current policy, the preservation of ethnic identity is a *voluntary* matter, both for the individual and for the group. The funding of multi-cultural programmes will, therefore, be directed *only* towards those ethnic groups whose members *express a desire* to maintain their ethno-cultural heritage and who can demonstrate a *need for support* in their efforts to maintain their ethnic distinctiveness. Similarly, Mr. Trudeau recognized the right of each individual to be *free to choose* whether or not to maintain his or her distinctive ethnic identity.

Unlike the ideal model of cultural pluralism which assumes that every individual and group desires to maintain a distinctive ethnic identity and heritage, the current Canadian policy of multi-culturalism, as espoused by Prime Minister Trudeau, gives recognition to the fact that some people will, inevitably, find greater human affinities *outside* their ethnic group than within it. Thus, while the policy legitimates the right of each "ethno-cultural" community to maintain its distinctiveness, it also gives recognition to the right of individuals to *choose* whether or not to value maintenance of ties and loyalties to their particular ethnic group and it supports the right of individuals to participate fully in Canadian society, independent of their (actual or assumed) ethnic classification. This protection of individual freedom may serve to reduce the disparities and temper the potential conflict between ethnic interest groups which a more rigidly pluralistic policy might engender.

Although the official policy of multi-culturalism, as stated by Prime Minister Trudeau, clearly represents a swing away from dominant conformity towards cultural pluralism, the programmes implemented, to-date, under its auspices are far less indicative of this trend. Their emphasis is on the preservation of *traditional* arts and crafts, and *traditional* ways of viewing and doing things ("folk" or "museum" culture) rather than upon the growth and development of *living, Canadian* cultures— the distinctive ethno-Canadian ways of life that have developed through the processes of integration into Canadian society. While the current multi-cultural policy may serve to differentiate Canadians from their U.S. neighbours by protecting their right to maintain ethnic group distinctiveness, it clearly fails, as implemented to-date, to provide more than minimally for Trudeau's "creative encounters" —the continuing face-to-face exchange of ideas, problems and solutions between members of different ethnic groupings—crucial to the development of a common and distinctive *Canadian national* consciousness and identity. Current multi-cultural programmes may serve, for some Canadians, to revive or strengthen *ethnic* identity and commitment, but they do not encourage large-scale, direct inter-ethnic exchange or the redistribution of resources necessary for greater minority penetration of majority institutions. In effect, they emphasize diversity and short-change national unity.

Multi-cultural policy of minority ethnic integration, is, in effect, a modified version of the (old) dominant group conformity model, now officially allowing for the persistence of the ancestral culture of ethnic minorities and unofficially ensuring that they are maintained in a subordinate position.

Implicit in both past and present Canadian models of dominant group conformity, is required acculturation for all ethnic minorities. In order to obtain the necessary skills and qualifications required by the majority for effective participation in the social institutions of the majority society, the minority ethnic member must acculturate, to the required degree, to the dominant Euro-Canadian pattern. But, in practice, both acculturation and assimilation are impeded to a degree commensurate with the visibility of the particular ethnic minority, by barriers of individual, institutional and structural racism. The more dissimilar the ethnic minority (in terms of physical, cultural and behavioural indices) from the majority ideal, the greater the discriminatory effects of racism implicit in the dominant group conformity model, and the greater the barriers to integration within Canadian society. Thus, for Canada's indigenous peoples, there is still no room at the top.

Chapter 10

The Transformation of Systems
of Ethnic Stratification

The concept of integration presupposes some degree of acceptance on the part of ethnic minorities of dominant group norms, values and goals. As long as some form of integration within the existing system is desired by most members of ethnic minorities, the established ethnic hierarchy remains unquestioned and unchallenged as a moral order. What is desired on the part of most members of ethnic minorities is upward social mobility within the ranks of the established order to enhance life chances. But in any system of social ranking, the potential for conflict, though not always overt, is nevertheless present. Even in the most stable system of ethnic stratification existing disparities in power, privilege and prestige, and inequalities in opportunities to acquire the skills which provide access to these values, generate bases for tension and conflict between majority and minority ethnic groupings. However, as long as most members of ethnic minorities are reasonably satisfied with their "place" and as long as they are prevented from acquiring competitive advantages which bring them into direct power struggles with the majority group(s), the system of ethnic stratification is not forced openly into critical question.

SOURCES OF OVERT CONFLICT: CHANGING LIFE CONDITIONS

Inter-ethnic conflict develops when life conditions change suddenly or radically so as to provide new alternatives, new hopes, and new competitive advantages for members of ethnic minorities. Such major changes in life conditions may be a result of external forces emanating from outside a community or society. Natural disasters such as floods, famine or disease may wipe out entire communities or entire populations. Similarly, human atrocities such as war and conquest may upset the demographic balance, as well as the relative balance of power between the ethnic groups in contact. An outstanding Canadian case-in-point is provided by the Beothuk Indians, the indigenous inhabitants of Newfoundland, who were completely extinguished by 1829, largely through continued raids and massacres at the hands of French settlers (McDiarmid & Pratt, 1971, pp. 64-65).

Scientific, Economic and Technological Developments. Today, with increasing modernization, urbanization and industrialization of communities and societies throughout the world, scientific, economic and technological developments have emerged as major forces of inter-ethnic conflict and change. In a modern nation such as Canada, there is a growing demand for new skills and abilities and a diminishing demand for traditional ones. Education becomes increasingly important as the demand for highly skilled specialists increases and the need for unskilled labour decreases. When members of ethnic minorities acquire new skills which are crucial to the economy they become of vital importance to the labour force. Similarly, when ethnic minorities gain purchasing power or bargaining power, they acquire new competitive advantages.

The findings of a recent study conducted by Dr. Merrijoy Kelner (1969) indicate that representation of minority ethnics in the Toronto elite structure has grown considerably since World War II. In general, the pioneer fields which had no entrenched majority elite in control, and those requiring a high degree of scientific and technological specialization, such as construction, the new universities, the new professions and mining were found to be most open to minority ethnics. To-date, Jews have been the most successful of the various ethnic minority groups in penetrating the elite structure of Toronto. Kelner suggests that their present success can be attributed to their length of residence in the community as well as their high educational achievements and traditional urban background.

Kelner reports that, in contrast to ethnic majority leaders who typically achieved wealth and influence by rising within the established bureaucratic structures, minority ethnics typically achieved prominence outside of the established majority institutions, through more individualistic and high-risk paths. A common "route to the top" for members of both the Jewish and Italian ethnic minorities, was to start one's own business or firm, employing and servicing fellow ethnics, and to build it into an important corporate structure. In this way, ethnic institutions developed within minority ethnic communities were able to grow, expand, and eventually gain competitive advantages vis-à-vis majority institutions. To ensure success in competition with majority institutions, certain techniques of "anglicization" were often employed by minority ethnic entrepreneurs. It was customary, for example, for such entrepreneurs to co-opt representation of at least a token few majority group members, whose names, added to the roster of the board of directors of a minority ethnic institution, ensured legitimation for the business or professional enterprise within the majority community.

Changes in Population Composition. Life conditions often alter radically as a result of various kinds of migration in or out of a community. The influx of new ethnic groups and the exodus of others, rural/urban migration, and shifts due to transient or migrant labour can result in important demographic changes. Changes in population composition can, in turn, result in alterations in the relative position of different ethnic groupings within the overall hierarchy.

As a consequence of immigration, particularly since World War II, Canada has become increasingly multi-ethnic in population composition. According to the 1971 Census, ethnic groups other than British and French represent more than a quarter of the post-war population (26.7%). Post-war immigration has affected the population composition of some regions far more than others. For example, although Ontario contains only about one-third of the population of Canada, it has received more than half of all post-war immigrants. In addition, these new immigrants tend to be attracted to the larger urban centres where economic opportunities appear to be most plentiful.

Metropolitan Toronto has attracted more than one-third of all post-war immigrants to Canada. As a result, the population composition has changed radically. Until 1945, the population of Toronto was overwhelmingly "White", British and Protestant in composition. Today, the community is among the most multi-ethnic in Canada, with over one-third of the population of non-British origin. This change in population composition has, in turn, resulted in changes in the proportionate representation of various ethnic groups within Toronto's elite structure. Kelner's study carried out in the late 1960's, clearly demonstrates that representation of minority ethnics in positions of influence and leadership within the major educational, economic, political and cultural institutions of the majority community has risen considerably since World War II. Jews were found to be represented significantly in the cultural sphere of leadership, while Italians and Ukrainians were (increasingly) represented in the sphere of labour leadership. In addition, a wide variety of members of other ethnic minorities were gaining prominence in positions of leadership in the research and planning branches of the Civil Service.

Although there has been penetration of ethnic minorities in nearly all the secondary institutions of the majority community, in no field has the *proportion* of minority ethnics in the elite reached the same level as that of the (respective) ethnic population in the city. The proportion of minority ethnics in Toronto, at the time of Kelner's study was about 40 per cent, but only seven per cent of Toronto's corporate elite was found to be represented by members of ethnic minorities.

Developments in Transportation and Communication. One of the major modern developments affecting inter-ethnic relations on a global scale is the tremendous advance in the fields of transportation and communication. Whether through travel or tele-communication the minority ethnic member is, today, increasingly exposed to a plethora of new values, ideas and standards which challenge traditional ways. With the recent (1972) launching of Anik, the new Canadian Satellite, even the most remote Inuit community in the High Arctic now receives (or will shortly receive) radio and telephone communication, and the larger settlements such as Frobisher Bay will receive television programmes from southern Canada. This development could have massive potential for socio-cultural change. Exposure to new ideas and values brings rising expectations and comparisons with other ethnic minorities who have improved their status. As a result, members of indigenous minorities may become critical of the existing hierarchy and discontented with their lowly position in it.

Increased opportunities for communication through travel, has recently been provided Canada's indigenous peoples through government funding of Indian and Inuit socio-political organizations. Conferences and meetings now bring together representatives of previously isolated communities and provide a new opportunity for exchange of ideas, goals and, most importantly, strategies for achieving desired goals. A prime example is provided by the recent coalition of six organizations of indigenous Canadian peoples, Indian, Inuit and Métis, affected by the proposed Mackenzie Valley natural gas pipeline. The purpose of the new organization is to set up a common front to bargain for settlement of various indigenous land claims with the federal government of Canada. The recent success of the Alaskan indigenous peoples in obtaining a substantial settlement for aboriginal land claims from the United States Government, has provided a major impetus for similar actions on the part of organizations of Canadian indigenous peoples; a point clearly demonstrated by the inclusion of the Alaskan Federation of Natives as an "affiliate" in the new Canadian "Federation of Natives North of 60 Degrees". Moreover, the president of the Alaskan Federation of Natives flew to the organizational meeting at Whitehorse, Northwest Territories, to urge the Canadian groups to demand a negotiated political settlement of their claims on the Alaskan model (*Akwesasne Notes*, 1972).

Provision of successful models for minorities throughout the world to emulate, is becoming a crucial aspect of modern communication. The achievement of independence and nationhood by indigenous peoples throughout Africa has had a marked influence on the development of Black Nationalism in the United States. Similarly, Black Power movements in the United States and the West Indies have sparked parallel activities among certain segments of the Black minority in Canada, especially the urban young. Black Power has, in turn, been paralleled by Red (Indian) Power movements both within the United States and Canada; and, in French Canada, the members of the F.L.Q. (Front de Libération du Québec) have identified themselves as the alleged "White Niggers of America" (Vallières, 1971).

Education. In a modern industrial society such as Canada, the most important channel of upward social mobility within the system of ethnic stratification is education. Direct competition between members of majority and minority ethnic groups in the public sphere, facilitates the upward mobility of the most highly educated, skilled and talented members of ethnic minorities. Through higher education, (these) minority ethnics learn not only new skills, but new ideas and values. As they gain competitive advantages and acquire wealth and power, members of ethnic minorities are often no longer willing to accept derogatory labelling and treatment in terms of ethnic stereotypes, nor are they willing to accept subordinate roles.

Inter-ethnic conflict develops when highly qualified

members of ethnic minorities are denied access to decision-making positions within the majority society, and/or denied entrance into the private social clubs and cliques of the majority ethnic group. Members of the dominant ethnic group are usually willing to grant some degree of formal acceptance to highly educated and skilled members of ethnic minorities in the public sphere of secondary social institutions, but informal acceptance in the private sphere of majority clubs and cliques lags far behind. This "status inconsistency"— the discrepancy between greatly increased levels of power and privilege, and a continuing low level of prestige—is what often leads to both personal and social conflict among mobile members of ethnic minorities.

Dr. Kelner, in her investigation of Toronto's elite structure, distinguished between two levels of elite status: a. The *Strategic Elite*, consisting of persons who had attained key functional positions in Canadian society and/or had acquired a reputation for outstanding achievement in a particular institutional sphere. b. The *Core Elite*, consisting of persons who not only belonged to the strategic elite, but were also accorded the highest degree of prestige in the community. The core elite represents the "super elite", at the apex of the elite structure, whose members rank highest in power, privilege and prestige.

The inability of minority ethnic members of the various strategic elites (labour, politics, government, professional, academic, celebrity, etc.) to enter the ranks of the core elite was found to be primarily due to their failure to gain informal acceptance by Toronto's social leaders. A continuing high degree of social distance between majority and minority ethnic members of strategic elites was clearly demonstrated in the formal and categorical nature of social relationships between members of the two groups. The majority members typically viewed the minority members as representatives of their ethnic groups, rather than as individuals and equals. Although minority ethnic members of strategic elites tended to be highly assimilated in the public sphere and to live and work side by side with majority members, they were rarely invited to join the exclusive social clubs of the majority or to participate in their intimate social gatherings. Kelner contends that it is this discrepancy between their high position in the public institutional sphere, and their lack of commensurate prestige in the private sphere, that prevents minority ethnic members of strategic elites from entering the core elite.

This social exclusion of minority ethnics has the effect of containing the highest level of power, privilege and prestige within a closed, upper class, "White", British, Protestant circle. Kelner indicates, for example, that membership in the leading men's clubs of the majority ethnic group is a tacit prerequisite for advancement to top positions in many fields, particularly in the professions and large corporations. It is in the relaxed, informal, club setting that many major decisions are made, and within the camaraderie of the private club or social gathering that young men are recognized and selected for future leadership roles. For the majority ethnic member, informal ties of friendship and kinship reinforce formal social links forged through common positions on commissions and boards. In this way the various aspects of the public and private spheres of life overlap and combine to extend the scope of power and prestige of dominant group members. In contrast, just as few informal ties of friendship and kinship exist between majority and minority members, formal social links are also rare. For minority ethnics, high achievement in one area does not often lead to positions of influence in other areas. Leadership status tends to be confined to the specific area of achievement because of ascriptive barriers, imposed by the dominant group, based on criteria of ethnicity, religion and socio-economic class, as well as lack of "appropriate" kinship and friendship "connections".

MARGINALITY AND THE ROLE OF THE MARGINAL
ETHNIC LEADER

The frustration and self-conflict experienced by minority ethnic mobiles who have been denied entrance into the private world of the dominant ethnic group, is often compounded through their rejection by fellow ethnics. Those members of ethnic minorities who have advanced far more quickly than other members of their group are often resented and attacked by their fellow ethnics who accuse them of "going over to the other side". Accordingly, minority ethnic mobiles typically become "marginal men", having a partial status in two ethnic worlds (minority and majority), but not fully accepting or fully accepted in either. Ethnic marginals are characteristically people with a status dilemma: they are caught between the push and pull forces of two incongruous reference groups, and experience great difficulty in meeting the inconsistent demands of both status audiences. They are in a position of confusion of social identity and are constantly faced with the question of primary ethnic identification and loyalty.

Resolution of the problem of marginality may take many forms. Sometimes ethnic marginals who have been rejected by the dominant group re-identify strongly with the minority group and become minority group leaders. Marginals may exploit their intermediate status by becoming arbitrators or mediators between the ethnic categories or they may become innovators, leaders of movements for social reform or revolution. Others, who have managed to achieve a limited degree of social acceptance by the majority, aspire to total acceptance and membership in the dominant ethnic group and persist in their attempts to completely assimilate.

Ethnic marginals play key roles in the transformation of a system of ethnic stratification; they are often the agents of change—the models who set the pace for fellow ethnics. As they move up the ethnic hierarchy and gain wealth, power and prestige, they can help to eliminate the traditional assumptions of inferiority associated with their ethnic category, and thus hasten the breakdown of negative ethnic stereotypes and the invisible wall built upon them.

The personal and social repercussions of marginality have been clearly demonstrated in Kelner's study of

Toronto elites. Kelner points out, that despite the general pattern of social exclusion, a few minority ethnic leaders in Toronto have gained admission into the core elite. This small group is composed for the most part of one or two highly assimilated Jews (whom Kelner calls "White Jews"), whose affiliations with the Jewish ethnic group are nominal, or non existent. In general, admission into the core elite, for minority ethnics, requires approximation as closely as possible to the upper class, "W.A.S.P." model. In order to successfully "blend" into the dominant elite establishment, the minority ethnic must relinquish or camouflage his distinctive ethnic identity. In effect, he must change both his reference group and membership group. He must fully identify with the dominant elite and participate exclusively in dominant group institutions and activities. As Kelner points out, this shift inevitably involves identification problems. The minority ethnic typically becomes a marginal man, not fully accepted by either minority or majority ethnic group. The dominant group attitude is that he is not "one of them" (an insider) and the minority group attitude is that he is disloyal and has repudiated his responsibility to his ethnic fellows. The pressures against assimilation were found to be particularly evident within the Jewish ethnic grouping, which provided the largest potential category of minority ethnic candidates for core elite status in Toronto.

Kelner found that, in general, close involvement with one's own ethnic group was not characteristic of the minority ethnic in Toronto's elite. This phenomenon was especially marked in contrast to those minority ethnics who held important positions of ethnic leadership within their own minority communities. The evidence indicates that the comparative restriction of minority ethnic leaders' activities to their own ethnic communities serves to reduce their chances of achieving elite status in the majority Toronto community. Kelner suggests that the hostile reaction of insiders may serve to "pull" assimilating members back into the fold. Their desire for leadership may then shift from majority to minority community. On the other hand, the assimilating minority ethnic may be "pushed" towards further penetration of majority elites. In the case of those minority ethnics who have already achieved dominant elite status within the Toronto community, mobility has been clearly associated with assimilation. Greater participation in the social institutions of the dominant community has been accompanied by a weakening of ties with the minority ethnic group.

Although the present representation of minority ethnics in the dominant core elite is "token", Kelner suggests that dominant ethnic group boundaries will become increasingly permeable under continuing pressure from the greater and greater numbers of minority ethnics represented in strategic elites. If the strategic level of elites continues to expand, as predicted, this development could have important implications for future patterns of minority ethnic integration in Canada. For example, one might predict, in the case of Torontonian Jews, that the present pluralistic pattern of integration would undergo considerable transformation as the number of peripherally-identified Jewish members of strategic and core (dominant) elites increases. This kind of prediction does not, and indeed cannot, take into account the crucial variable in this connection—the degree of willingness of the dominant group to allow and co-operate with the position adopted by the minority ethnic member. Both assimilationist and melting pot patterns depend on this kind of co-operation.

The model of integration adopted by the minority ethnic elite is of crucial importance in the transformation of a system of ethnic stratification. If the minority ethnic leadership favours dominant conformity as a strategy for penetration of the majority society, the chances for preservation of the identity and integrity of the minority ethnic grouping are curtailed. If, however, the minority ethnic leadership favours cultural pluralism, the chances for members uniting and taking concerted action in the interest of ethnic group preservation are enhanced. The particular response of the minority ethnic elite will, in any case, be predicated at least in part on the willingness or

unwillingness of the majority ethnic group to allow penetration of its social institutions by mobile minority ethnics.
Continued frustration of the assimilationist aspirations of
minority ethnic leaders, by barriers imposed from the
majority, may eventually lead to overt conflict between
minority and majority ethnic groups.

MINORITY RESPONSES TO INTER-ETHNIC CONFLICT

Overt conflict between majority and minority ethnic
viewpoints may result in responses of submission, contention or revitalization.

Submission results when the ethnic minority passively
accepts the inferior evaluation and status ascribed to it by
the dominant group(s). This response has, until recently,
been widespread among Canada's Indian and Black populations. In *contention*, the ethnic minority rejects the
inferior evaluation imposed upon it by the majority,
protests against its ascribed status and demands equality
and integration within the existing social order. Contention
may involve a pluralist response (equality and ethnic
separation) *or* an assimilationist response (equality and
ethnic extinction). Contemporary Canadian Indians are
divided in this respect: some favour the pluralist response
of leaders like Harold Cardinal (1971); while William
Wuttunee (1971) and his followers, favour full assimilation. A response of contention may lead over time to
organized movements for social and political reform by
members of ethnic minorities.

A *revitalization* response is most likely to develop when
there is a vast discrepancy between minority and majority
evaluations of minority ethnic status. A revitalization
movement is a particular form of minority ethnic protest
and arises under specific conditions of (perceived) oppression. It is most often a response to the experience of severe
cultural deprivation and represents an attempt on the
part of ethnic leadership to generate or regenerate a firm
sense of positive, ethnic self-identification among (previously) apathetic and/or alienated members of ethnic
minorities who had for a long time given up hope of self-

or ethnic group betterment. The theme of revitalization, whether couched in religious or secular terms, is *cultural transformation*. Its premises, strategies and goals, articulated in a clearly defined ideology, tend to portray the conflict between the minority ethnic group and its opponent(s), (the majority), as an historical/cosmic struggle between good (ethnic insiders) and evil (outsiders). The ideology of revitalization among ethnic minorities, not only denies the majority claim to superior status, but affirms the alleged moral and ethical superiority of the minority group. The majority is depicted as the evil oppressor and is blamed for the disabilities and sufferings (associated with the ascribed inferior status) of the allegedly "innocent" minority victims. Revitalization of "the good life" of the minority, (it is argued), necessitates the expulsion of evil, i.e. the elimination of the evil (majority) oppressors and the creation or re-creation of the "just society" by members of the ethnic minority *themselves*. Revitalization thus involves a deliberate, organized effort on the part of members of ethnic minorities to create a totally new, social and cultural world for themselves in accordance with their own values, goals and standards (Wallace, 1956). Revitalization may involve a politically revolutionary response, in which members of ethnic minorities attempt to overthrow the established social order or secede (separate) from it in order to build their own version of the truly just society. It may, on the other hand, lead to a reactionary *or* counter-revolutionary movement *or* to a response of total withdrawal from the existing social order through cultural secession or encapsulation.

The particular pattern of response adopted by a minority ethnic group may vary over time, with changing social conditions. A group which has traditionally been submissive may gain new competitive advantages and seek social reform (contention). If demands for reform are continually blocked, a revitalization orientation may develop, leading to the organization of political, revolutionary movements.

Canadian Indians have moved from a long-term response of submission to a contemporary response of contention under the active leadership of young, highly educated leaders such as Harold Cardinal and William Wuttunee. Wuttunee argues in favour of assimilation and in support of the federal government White Paper on Indian policy which proposes to phase out the "discriminatory" Indian Act as well as the Indian Affairs Branch and the reserve system, in favour of integration of Indians as full and equal citizens within the "mainstream" of Canadian Society (Government of Canada, 1969). Like Wuttunee, Cardinal argues against traditional policies of "wardship" legitimated under the Indian Act and carried out under the Department of Indian Affairs; but in opposition to Wuttunee he strongly opposes government policies aimed at full assimilation of Indians into Euro-Canadian society. Alternatively, Cardinal supports a pluralist position, arguing that Canadian Indians should determine their own future—their own role within Canadian society on their own terms and within the separate, institutional framework of Indian, ethnic organizations. Cardinal contends that the revitalization of the Indian cultural heritage is a necessary prerequisite to true acceptance of Indians as equals by the majority society and that such revitalization can only occur within a separate, Indian, socio-cultural context (Cardinal, 1969). Cardinal's model of the "just society", thus demands a minority response of revitalization and social segregation, in order to reach the long-range goal of cultural pluralism.

The Development of Minority Ethnic Protest. Discontent among members of a minority ethnic group is generally initially unfocussed. In order to make demands for change, minority discontent must be mobilized and directed towards a clearly-defined goal. When the existing system of ethnic stratification is perceived by more and more members of an ethnic minority as unjust and corrupt, "contrast conceptions" may develop in which the majority ethnic group is perceived as the evil enemy oppressor, and the minority as the good and innocent victim of majority oppression. Such contrast conceptions sharpen and rigidify ethnic stereotypes and provide moral justification for concerted, aggressive action by the minority against the alleged "enemy". In this way, contrast conceptions can serve to facilitate the mobilization, focussing and directing of minority discontent towards the majority group.

Movements for social reform generated within ethnic minorities may gain impetus from frustrated minority ethnic mobiles, who realistically assess their own chances for status improvement in terms of the advancement of their minority ethnic group as a whole. Thus, contention often develops when frustrated minority ethnic marginals, prevented from attaining majority ethnic status, re-identify strongly with their own ethnic group, assume (minority) leadership, and mobilize the discontent of the masses. Widespread discontent is generally initially mobilized in terms of reform movements whose leaders, desirous of enhancing their own social position, have a vested interest in the "status quo". Reformers support the ideals of the established order and thus can often rally support from both dominant and minority ethnic groups through mass appeals to public opinion. Attempts to overthrow the existing order or secede from it, do not usually occur until leaders of ethnic minorities have failed or given up hope of achieving desired reforms. They then may attempt to organize subversive, revolutionary movements utilizing illegal, violent tactics such as terrorism and guerilla warfare.

Among Canadian Indians, the more conservative leadership of social reformers such as Cardinal and Wuttunee, is increasingly being challenged by more radical Indian leaders and organizations bent on revitalization and revolution. The Native Alliance for Red Power (N.A.R.P.), influenced by the Black Power movement in the United States, is a small but growing organization of young Indians who reject the "White man's world" and consider impossible all forms of Indian integration into it. Red Power—separate and equal Indian status and nationhood —is viewed as the only viable goal for the Canadian "Red

Man". Successful achievement of this goal would mean that Canadian Indians, while residing within Canadian territory, would be independent of and separate from the majority Canadian society. They would have a separate Indian society organized and governed by Indians and operated according to the ideas, values and standards of Indian culture (Walsh, 1971, pp. 196-198; Wuttunee, 1971, Ch. 1).

The separatist movement among French Canadians in Quebec similarly views independence as the key to a new life (Jones, 1972, Ch. 4). Jones contends that Canadian separatism has been a theme within French-Canadian nationalism for at least a century and a half, but never before has it proliferated into such a wide variety of factions, from extreme right to extreme left-wing in platform. At the extreme left is the Parti Pris, a non-political movement of young intellectuals who consider both political and economic independence as necessary prerequisites for the liberation of French Canada from the purported "alienation" imposed by colonization and exploitation. In more romantic, idealistic terms their view of the good life involves the establishment of a "truly" just world in which man's fullest self-awareness and human potential could be realized. To this end, all acts are considered moral to the extent that they are effective in political and revolutionary terms. All means which assist in the realization of the end (a just and human world) are thereby justified.

The revolutionary ideology of the Parti Pris provides a *"raison d'être"* for a separatist French Canadian revitalization movement. The Parti Pris is not, however, a political grouping. It was the members of the terrorist Front de Libération du Québec (F.L.Q.) who turned the revolutionary philosophy of separatists such as the Parti Pris into an organized, subversive revolutionary revitalization movement, utilizing illegal, violent tactics in an attempt to overthrow the existing order. In their short, sensational history (from March to June of 1963) the F.L.Q. used bombings and murder as techniques of violence, allegedly designed to awaken and convince

French Canadians to fight for independence. The F.L.Q. proclaimed the belief that Quebec's independence would be achieved by the violent struggle of its workers and intellectuals against the so-called middle-class English and French bourgeoisie. As a revitalization movement, the goal of the F.L.Q. is an independent and socialist nation in which the language, traditions and culture of French Canadians can and will thrive (Jones, pp. 88-91).

The leadership of both N.A.R.P. and the F.L.Q., consists of young Canadian intellectuals, highly frustrated members of ethnic minorities, impatient with the alleged snail's pace at which social change in the interest of their particular ethnic group is occurring. As potential revitalization movements, both groups claim to be inspired by a long-range goal: their version of the truly just society. Both consider any means towards achievement of their end (the good life/just society) to be viable. For the F.L.Q., violence is a built-in tactic; for N.A.R.P., it is a technique which (it is proclaimed) will be used, *if necessary*.

Revitalization movements are not *necessarily* violent, political or revolutionary in orientation. When demands for reform are continually and effectively blocked by the majority, the ethnic minority may adopt an introverted response. Instead of trying to change the established order, they withdraw from it and put their efforts into building a new and better world within the geographical and social confines of their own ethnic grouping. Such revitalization movements, which favour cultural encapsulation, are often religious and reactionary in orientation. Such introverted revitalization movements are typically sparked by *charismatic* rather than *elite* leaders. The authority of the charismatic leader unlike his elite counterpart, does not rest on his (recognized) social status. Rather, his authority derives from a special quality of personality, a (recognized) personal power of extraordinary magnetism which attracts or "pulls" his followers to him. Charismatic leaders may arise from within either parallel (congruent) or alternate (incongruent) status

systems of a minority community, but because the introverted revitalization movement is likely to be religious
and reactionary in orientation, charismatic leadership will
most probably be generated from within the traditional,
alternate system. Following from this, one may hypothe-
size that a minority ethnic community, under conditions
of inter-ethnic conflict, will be more likely to generate
extroverted (reform and revolutionary) revitalization
responses, under assimilationist/elite leaders developed
within parallel institutions; and more likely to generate
introverted (encapsulation) responses under traditional-
ist/charismatic leaders developed within alternate institutions.

A major problem, deriving from the nature of charismatic leadership, is what Max Weber has termed "routin-
ization of charisma". Initially, followers of a charismatic
leader are drawn to the movement more through emotional
commitment to the leader, than through ideological
commitment to the "cause". It is, therefore, of the utmost
importance that the initial, *personal power* of the leader
be converted into the *authority of office* within a stable
(ongoing) institutional framework.

The process by which this is accomplished ("routiniza-
tion of charisma") is a critical issue in movement organization; for if it does *not* occur, leadership authority cannot
be delegated and distributed to other personnel, and the
movement itself may die with the death or failure of its
original leader.

Although religious revitalization movements are sometimes transformed into revolutionary movements, initially
they do not threaten the established social order. They
are essentially safety-valve mechanisms, providing members of the ethnic minority with displacement techniques
through which they can project the blame for their perceived or actual misfortunes, onto the dominant group.
Thus, religious revitalization movements provide a cath-
artic outlet for the release of minority ethnic tensions and
frustrations. Whether or not revitalization movements
will develop revolutionary tendencies depends largely on

the relative power of the majority and minority ethnic groups, as well as on the degree of coercion backing the superior power of the dominant group. Where the power discrepancy and the coercive means of its enforcement are great, revolutionary tendencies are usually effectively constrained.

Both the Hutterites and Doukhobors are religious sects which began as religious revitalization movements. Members of both groups were, initially, drawn away from established Christian churches by charismatic leaders who convinced them to "live the good life" based upon communal and pacifist ideals. Both groups rejected the "outside world", viewed as enemy oppressors, and both were initially religious, reactionary and introverted in orientation. In Canada, the Hutterites (as previously discussed) have successfully maintained their initial strategy of encapsulation and have become economically self-sufficient. They have effectively "routinized" the authority of leadership and have developed a stable, institutionalized leadership pattern. The Doukhobors, on the other hand, have had less success in encapsulating themselves and in becoming self-sufficient. They have been unsuccessful in developing a stable leadership structure, and, upon the death of their charismatic, immigrant leader, in Canada, the Doukhobor community became divided into several factions, some of which are more violent and revolutionary in orientation than others.

The Sons of Freedom is a militant Doukhobor group in British Columbia whose once prosperous farms and villages have become poverty-ridden and whose co-operative enterprises have been replaced by casual jobs and government handouts. The Sons of Freedom utilize violent techniques such as arson to terrorize neighbours and government authorities and to draw public attention to alleged "long overlooked abuses" (Davis & Krauter, 1971, pp. 81-85). They use sensationalism in such activities as nude marches, both to attract attention to their cause and to deliberately flout the alleged moral code of the "outside world", which they view as immoral. Through more violent means such as burnings and bombings they demonstrate their vehement rejection of the (supposedly) materialistic/hedonistic value system of Euro-Canadian society. Despite the fact that militant Doukhobor demonstrations are explicitly political in thrust, their revolutionary gains, achieved by attracting public attention through the mass media are often more than nullified by the repression which follows their violent activities.

As the fate of the F.L.Q. clearly demonstrates, it is highly unlikely, given the (present) super-ordinate power of the Euro-Canadian majority, that a violent, revolutionary movement generated within a Canadian ethnic minority will achieve more than temporary gains in any attempt to activate its philosophy. As long as the power discrepancy between the majority and minority ethnic groups remain high, the long-range repercussions of sporadic bombings, burnings or murders, will be to effectively repress, and probably destroy the revolutionary movements responsible.

Summary. Minority ethnic protest may be interpreted largely as a reaction to racism. It is usually rooted in a long-term experience of injustice, inequality and perceived oppression, predicated on assumed "racial" inferiority. Attempts on the part of ethnic minorities to gain equal access to power, privilege and prestige, whether through social reform or revolution, must therefore, seek to eradicate the racist premises upon which the existing ethnic stratification system operates. Thus, the success of any organized form of minority ethnic protest will inevitably involve a change in the *criteria* for stratification, from ascribed characteristics (such as ethnicity or so-called "race") to those based on achievement (such as skill or education). What this implies is that a *fully successful* minority ethnic protest movement would result in the complete transformation of the system of ethnic stratification from an ethnic to a socio-economic, class-based hierarchy, *or* more radically, from an ethnic ranking system to a "classless" society. The latter would involve more than a change in *criteria* for ranking, it would involve the elimination of *ranking* itself.

In Canada, prospects for this kind of transformation

are, at present, dim. Despite persistent myths of "class-lessness" i.e. middle-class equality of possessions (Porter, 1965, pp. 3-7), and of the egalitarian mosaic (ethnic equality of opportunity), the vertical structure of ethnic inequality remains relatively impervious to minority ethnic protest. The truly "just society" remains a Canadian dream.

Chapter 11
Whither Canadians?
Problems and Prospects

Canadians have long prided themselves on being citizens of a country which has no "race problem". The Canadian national self-image has, from the beginning, been that of a tolerant, law-abiding nation dedicated in practice, as in ideology, to democracy and peace. Geographical proximity to the United States, a nation actively engaged in the "race war" (Segal, 1966)—the global colour-conflict between the established powers and the "Third World"—both at home and abroad, has reinforced these ethnocentric notions. Violent confrontation between Black and White in the urban inner-cities of the United States, compounded by a seemingly endless Vietnam War, has generated a typically "quiet" Canadian response of self-congratulation. The Canadian man on the street *knows* that "we have no Black problem", and thinks that the Vietnam War is "inhuman, immoral, and certainly un-Canadian". In other words, Canadians, consciously or unconsciously, attempt to boost their feelings of self-and national identity by contraposing their "peaceful and just society" to that of their "violent and racist" neighbour to the south.

Ironically, it has been the recent post-war immigration of American and West Indian Blacks to Canada that has brought to the fore the latent racism within the Canadian stratification system. When questioned as to their experience of prejudice and discrimination in Canada, vis-à-vis the United States, recent Black immigrants have suggested that the difference is a subtle one (*Toronto Daily Star*, 1972). Canadians, it appears, are "polite racists". They *politely* move slightly away from a Black co-passenger on the subway; they *politely* refuse to rent to or hire a Black; they *politely* refer to Blacks as negroes rather than "niggers", and in general, they *politely* continue to discriminate against and segregate themselves from all but the most impersonal, formal contacts with their Black fellow (or potential fellow) Canadian citizens.

Of course, one could repeat the story for all "visible" minorities: Indians, Métis and Inuit, Chinese, Japanese, etc. The point is that racism, whether overt or covert, polite or rude, is as deeply rooted in the Canadian hierarchy of ethnic inequality as it is in the American system. Despite a post-World War II proliferation of human rights legislation both at the federal and provincial levels, as well as a marked increase in positive governmental activities (especially the funding of minority ethnic organizations), structural and institutional forms of racism against ethnic minorities, particularly those defined in racial terms, persists in Canada today. If our struggle towards full observance of human rights and fundamental freedoms throughout Canada is to be given more than lip service, we, as Canadian citizens, must insist upon and work for consistent *enforcement* of anti-racist legislation; and we must take upon ourselves the crucial responsibility for educating our children towards the spirit of human rights: we must *demonstrate* in our own public and private lives, that "race" does not define "place" in the truly just society.

References

Chapter 1. The Spectrum of
Man and His Diversity
COUNT, E. W., *This is Race*,
New York, Henry Schuman,
1950.
MAYR, E., *Animal Species and
Evolution*, Cambridge,
Mass., Belknap Press, 1963.
HOOTON, E. A., *Up from the
Ape*, rev. ed., New York,
Macmillan, 1946.
BOYD, W. C., *Genetics and the
Races of Man*, Boston, Little,
Brown, 1950.

Chapter 2. The Evolution of
Man and the Origin of
Races"
SIMONS, E. L. & PILBEAM, D. R.,
"Preliminary Revision of the
Dryopithecinae" (Pongidae,
Anthropoidea)", *Folia.
Primat.*, #3, 81.
PILBEAM, D., *The Ascent of
Man*, New York, Macmillan,
1972.

Chapter 3. Inheritance, En-
vironment and Human
Adaptability
LINNE, C. von, *A General
System of Nature, Through
the Three Grand Kingdoms
of Animals, Vegetables, and
Minerals, Systematically
Divided into their Several
Classes, Orders, Genera,
Species and Varieties, with
their Habitations, Manners,
Economy, Structure, and
Peculiarities*, Translated by
William Turton, London,
Lackington & Allen & Co.,
1806.
STERN, C., *Principles of
Human Genetics*, San
Francisco and New York,
Freeman & Co., 1960.

Chapter 4. Race and
Intelligence
HAWTHORN, H. B. (ed.), *A
Survey of the Contemporary
Indians of Canada*, Vol. 2,
Ottawa, Queen's Printer,
1967.
CLARK, BARBARA S., *Child
Study*, Vol. 29, No. 3; Vol.
29, No. 4, 1967.
RICHARDSON, K. & SPEARS, D.
(eds.), *Race and Intelli-
gence*, Penguin Books,
Baltimore, 1972.

Chapter 5. The Peoples of
Canada Today
SHAPIRO, H. L., *The Jewish
People*, UNESCO, Paris,
1960.
SLOBODIN, R., "Métis of the
Far North", in ELLIOT, J. L.
(ed.) *Native Peoples*, Vol. 1;
Minority Canadians,
Prentice-Hall of Canada,
Scarborough, 1971.
HUGHES, D. R. & BROTHWELL,
D. R., 1970, "The Earliest
Populations of Man in
Europe, Western Asia and
North Africa", being Chapter
5, pp. 156-172, in Edwards,
I. E. S., Gadd, G. J. &
N. L. G. Hammond, (eds.)
*The Cambridge Ancient
History*, 3rd edition, Vol. 1,
Part 1, Cambridge,
The University Press.

Chapter 6. Race, Racism
and Ethnicity
DAVIS, M., and KRAUTER, J. F.,
The Other Canadians,
Toronto, Methuen, 1971.
HALL, CAPTAIN C. S., *Life
with the Esquimaux*,
Edmonton, M. G. Hurtig
Limited, 1970.
HAWTHORN, H. B. (ed.), *A
Survey of the Contemporary
Indians of Canada*, Vol. 2,
Ottawa, Queen's Printer,
1967.
HUGHES, C. C., "Under Four
Flags: Recent Culture
Change Among the Eski-
mos", in *Current Anthro-
pology*, Vol. 6, No. 1, pp.
3-73, February, 1965.
Indian Act (Office Consoli-
dation), Ottawa, Queen's
Printer, 1965.
KALLEN, E. (*in press*), Span-
ning the Generations: A
Comparative Study of Ex-
pressions of Jewish Identity
among Adults and Youth in
Toronto, to be published *in*
Proceedings of the Sixth
World Congress of Jewish
Studies, Vol. 7,
Jerusalem, Israel.
KELNER, M., "Ethnic Penetra-
tion into Toronto's Elite
Structure", in *Canadian
Review of Sociology and
Anthropology*, 7:2, pp.
128-137, 1970.
MCDIARMID, G., and PRATT, D.,
Teaching Prejudice, Toronto,
OISE (Ontario Institute for
Studies in Education), 1971.
PORTER, J., *The Vertical
Mosaic*, Toronto, University
of Toronto Press, 1965.

RICHMOND, A., "Immigration and Pluralism in Canada", in Mann, W. E., (ed.), *Social and Cultural Change in Canada*, Vol. 1, Toronto, Copp Clark, pp. 81-96, 1970. Language, Ethnicity and the Problem of Identity in a Canadian Metropolis, a paper presented at the IXth International Congress of Anthropological and Ethnological Sciences, Chicago, Aug. 28-Sept. 8, 1973.

ROSE, T. I., *The Subject is Race*, New York, Oxford University Press, 1968.

WALSH, G., *Indians in Transition*, Toronto, McClelland and Stewart, 1971.

WRONG, D. H., "Ontario's Jews in the Larger Community" in Rose, A. (ed.) *A People and its Faith*, Toronto, University of Toronto Press, pp. 46-47, 1959.

YETMAN, M. R., and STEELE, C. H., *Majority and Minority: the Dynamics of Racial and Ethnic Relations*, Boston, Allyn and Bacon, 1971.

Chapter 7. Origin and Development of Ethnic Stratification

BALIKCI, A., *The Netsilik Eskimo*, Garden City, New York, American Museum of Natural History, Natural History Press, 1970.

BARTH, F., *Ethnic Groups and Boundaries*, Boston, Little, Brown and Company, 1969.

BRETON, R., "Institutional Completeness of Ethnic Communities and the Personal Relations of Immigrants", in *Canadian Society: Sociological Perspectives*, Blishen, B. R., et al., (eds.) Toronto, MacMillan of Canada, 1971.

CARDINAL, H., "The Unjust Society: the Tragedy of Canada's Indians", in Elliott, J. L., (ed.), *Minority Canadians 1: Native Peoples*, pp. 134-149, 1971.

JOY, R. J., *Languages in Conflict*, Toronto, McClelland and Stewart, 1972.

KELNER, M., The Elite Structure of Toronto: Ethnic Composition and Patterns of Recruitment, Department of Sociology, University of Toronto (Unpublished Ph.D. dissertation), 1969.

LEWIN, K., *Resolving Social Conflicts*, New York, Harper and Brother, 1948.

NOEL, D. L., "A Theory of the Origin of Ethnic Stratification" *in* Yetman, N. R., and Steele, C. H., *Majority and Minority*, Boston, Allyn and Bacon, pp. 32-50, 1971.

PORTER, J., *The Vertical Mosaic*, Toronto, University of Toronto Press, 1965.

RICHMOND, A., "Immigration and Pluralism in Canada," in

Mann, W. E., (ed.), *Social and Cultural Change in Canada*, Vol. 1, Toronto, Copp Clark, pp. 81-96, 1970.
The Toronto Star, Series of articles *on* Toronto's Black Community, September 9-13, 1972.
VANSTONE, J. W., "Influence of European Man on the Eskimos" in Steensel M. Van, (ed.), *People of Light and Dark*, Department of Indians Affairs and Northern Development, Ottawa, Information Canada, 1971.
WINKS, R. W., "The Canadian Negro: The Problem of Identity" in Elliott, J. L., (ed.), *Minority Canadians 2: Immigrant Groups*, pp. 95-105, 1971.

Chapter 8. The Persistence of Systems of Ethnic Stratification

ATNIKOV, P., OLESON, I. J., and MCRUER, G., "A Study of Social Studies Textbooks Approved for Use in Manitoba Schools", for the Manitoba Human Rights Commission, Manitoba Department of Youth and Education, Student Employment Programme, Winnipeg, Manitoba, 1964.
CLAIRMONT, D. H., and MAGILL, D. W., *Nova Scotian Blacks: An Historical and Structural Overview*, Halifax, Institute of Public Affairs, Dalhousie University, 1970.
DAILEY, R. C. and DAILEY, L. A., *The Eskimo of Rankin Inlet: A Preliminary Report*, Ottawa, Northern Coordination and Research Center, Department of Northern Affairs and Research Resources, 1961.
DAVIS, M. and KRAUTER, J. F., *The Other Canadians*, Toronto, Methuen, 1971.
Department of Indian Affairs and Northern Development, Report on Textbooks, Ottawa, February, 1969.
ELKIN, F., *The Employment of Visible Minority Groups in Mass Media Advertising*, for the Ontario Human Rights Commission, 1972.
HAWTHORN, H. B., *A Survey of the Contemporary Indians of Canada*, Vol. 2, Ottawa, Queen's Printer, 1967.
HOBART, C. W., "Eskimo Education in the Canadian Arctic", in *The Canadian Review of Sociology and Anthropology*, VII:I, pp. 49, 69, February, 1970.
HUGHES, E. C., *French Canada in Transition*, Chicago, University of Chicago, 1943.
Indian and Métis Conference, Committee of the Community Welfare Planning Council, *Survey of Canadian History Textbooks*, a Brief to the

Manitoba Department of Education, 1964.

JENNESS, D., *Eskimo Administration II, Canada*, Arctic Institute of North America, Technical Paper No. 14, May, 1964.

KEYFITZ, N., "Canadians and Canadiens" *in* Mann, W. E. (ed.), *Canada: A Sociological Profile*, Toronto, Copp Clark, pp. 168-178, 1968.

MCDIARMID, G. and PRATT, D., *Teaching Prejudice*, Toronto, Ontario Institute for Studies in Education, 1971.

SMILEY, D. V., *Canada in Question*, Toronto, McGraw-Hill, Ryerson Limited, 1972.

VALLEE, S. G., "Differentiation Among the Eskimo in Some Canadian Arctic Settlements" in Valentine, V. S. and Vallee, S. G. (eds.), *Eskimo of the Canadian Arctic*, Toronto, McClelland and Stewart Limited, 1968.

Chapter 9. Processes of Ethnic Integration

ELLIOTT, J. L. (ed.), *Minority Canadians I: Native Peoples*, Scarborough, Prentice Hall of Canada, 1971.

ELLIS, C. D., "Influence of the Missionary" in Steensel, *People of Light and Dark*, pp. 14-19, 1971.

FERGUSON, J., "Eskimos in a Satellite Society", in Steensel, pp. 14-19, 1971.

GANS, H. J., *The Urban Villagers*, New York, Free Press, 1962.

GLAZER, N. and MOYNIHAN, D. T., *Beyond the Melting Pot*, Cambridge, Massachusetts, MIT Press, 1963.

HONIGMANN, J. *and* I., "The Eskimo of Frobisher Bay", in Elliott, pp. 55-74, 1971.

HUGHES, C. C., Under Four Flags: "Recent Culture Change Among the Eskimo", in *Current Anthropology*, Vol. 6, No. 1, pp. 3-69, February 1965.

JANSEN, C. J., "Leadership in the Toronto Italian Ethnic Group", in *International Migration Review*, Vol. 4, Fall, 1969.

"The Italian Community in Toronto", in Elliott, pp. 207-215, 1971.

KELNER, M., "Ethnic Penetration into Toronto's Elite Structure", in *Canadian Review of Sociology and Anthropology*, 7:2, 1970.

LATOWSKY, E. (*Kallen*), "Family Lifestyles and Jewish Culture", in Ishwaran, K. (ed.), *The Canadian Family*, Toronto, Holt, Rinehart and Winston, 1971.

Eskimo Youth: The New Marginals in International Biological Programme, Human Adaptability Project (Igloolik, N.W.T.), Report No. 4, University of Toronto, 1971-1972.

RICHMOND, A. H., Immigrants and Ethnic Groups in Metropolitan Toronto, York University, Ethnic Research Programme, Institute for Behavioural Research, June, 1967.
Ethnic Segregation in Metropolitan Toronto, York University, Ethnic Research Programme, Institute for Behavioural Research, February, 1972.
ROSENBERG, S. E., *The Jewish Community in Canada*, Vols. 1 and 2, Toronto/Montreal, McClelland and Stewart, 1971.
SKLARE, M., *America's Jews*, N.Y., Random House, 1971.
STEENSEL, M. VAN (ed.), *People of Light and Dark*, Ottawa, Department of Indian Affairs and Northern Development, 1971.
VALENTINE, V. F., "The Forgotten People", in Steensel, pp. 110-114, 1971.
VALENTINE, V. F. and VALLEE, F. G. (eds.), *Eskimo of the Canadian Arctic*, Toronto, McClelland and Stewart, 1971.
VALLEE, F. G., "Differentiation Among the Eskimo in Some Canadian Arctic Settlements", in Valentine and Vallee, pp. 109-126.
"Eskimos of Canada as a Minority Group", in Elliott, pp. 75-88, 1971[a].
VRANAS, G. J. and STEPHENS, M., "The Eskimo of

Churchill Manitoba", in Elliott, pp. 29-54, 1971.
WERBLOWSKY, R. J. Z. and WIGODER, G., *The Encyclopedia of the Jewish Religion*, Canada, Holt, Rinehart and Winston, 1965.
WOODSWORTH, J. F., *Strangers Within Our Gates*, Toronto, University of Toronto Press, 1972.
ZIEGLER, F. (in association with RICHMOND, A. H.), Characteristics of Italian Householders in Metropolitan Toronto, York University, Ethnic Research Programme, Institute for Behavioural Research, February, 1972.

Chapter 10. The Transformation of Systems of Ethnic Stratification
Akwesasne Notes, "Native Peoples of the North Unite to Fight MacKenzie Pipeline", p. 36, Late autumn 1972.
CARDINAL, H., *The Unjust Society*, Edmonton, M. G. Hurtig, 1969.
DAVIS, M. & KRAUTER, J. F., *The Other Canadians*, Toronto, Methuen, 1971.
Government of Canada, *Statement on Indian Policy*, Queen's Printer, Catalogue No. R 32-2469, 1969.
JONES, R., *Community in Crisis*, Toronto, McClelland & Stewart, 1972.

KELNER, M., *The Elite Structure of Toronto: Ethnic Composition and Patterns of Recruitment*, Unpublished Ph.D. Dissertation, Department of Sociology, University of Toronto, 1969.

KUROKAWA, M., (ed.) *Minority Responses*, New York, Random House, 1970.

MCDIARMID, G. & PRATT, D., *Teaching Prejudice*, Toronto, Ontario Institute for Studies in Education, 1971.

PORTER, J., *The Vertical Mosaic*, Toronto, U. of Toronto Press, 1965.

VALLIÈRES, P., *White Niggers of America*, Toronto, McClelland & Stewart, 1971.

WALLACE, A. F. C., "Revitalization Movements", *in American Anthropologist*, Vol. 58, April, 1956.

WALSH, G., *Indians in Transition*, Toronto, McClelland & Stewart, 1971.

WUTTUNEE, W. I. C., *Ruffled Feathers*, Calgary, Alberta, Bell Books Ltd., 1971.

Chapter 11. Whither Canadians? Problems and Prospects

SEGAL, R., *The Race War*, London, Jonathan Cape, 1966.

Toronto Daily Star, Series on Metropolitan Toronto's Black Community, September 9-13, 1972.

Index